Victoria's Daughters

The Colourful Personal Lives of Queen Victoria's Five Daughters

Illustrated with Portraits from the Author's Collection

SUSAN SYMONS

Fascinating Royal History

Published by Roseland Books
The Old Rectory, St Just-in-Roseland, Truro, Cornwall, TR2 5JD
www.susansymons.com

ISBN: 978-1-8383845-2-4

For Abigail and Emily – talented and delightful granddaughters

CONTENTS

1

INTRODUCTION

On 28 August 1945 the coffin of Her Royal Highness the Princess Beatrice was interred in the village church at Whippingham near Osborne House on the Isle of Wight. Her son and his wife were the only mourners at the interment service. The princess had died at her niece's home on the British mainland the year before and her funeral held in St George's Chapel, Windsor Castle. With World War II in Europe now over her remains could be brought back to the Isle of Wight, the place Beatrice loved the most and regarded as home. Beatrice was the youngest of the five daughters of Queen Victoria and the last to die. A century separated the birth of Victoria's eldest daughter on 21 November 1840 and the death of Beatrice on 26 October 1944.

Victoria's five daughters were Victoria (born 1840), Alice (1843), Helena (1846), Louise (1848), and Beatrice (1857). The eldest married and left home when the youngest was less than a year old and they hardly knew each other as children. The five princesses were born into a world of privilege and deference, cocooned by their high rank and wealth. But their lives were fractured by the early death of their father, Prince Albert, and then dominated by the selfish demands of their controlling mother. Victoria's daughters were important public

Queen Victoria's five daughters

Victoria (Vicky) Princess Royal of Great Britain, Queen of Prussia, German Empress
Born 21 November 1840
Married 1858 Friedrich Wilhelm (Fritz) of Prussia (1831-1888)
King and queen of Prussia; German emperor and empress 1888
Eight children: four girls and four boys
Died 5 August 1901 Kronberg im Taunus, Frankfurt, Germany

Alice Grand Duchess of Hesse-Darmstadt
Born 25 April 1843
Married 1862 Ludwig (Louis) of Hesse-Darmstadt (1837-1892)
Grand duke and duchess of Hesse-Darmstadt 1877
Seven children: five girls and two boys
Died 14 December 1878 Darmstadt, Germany

Helena (Lenchen) Princess Christian of Schleswig-Holstein
Born 25 May 1846
Married 1866 Christian of Schleswig-Holstein (1831-1917)
Five children: two girls and three boys
Died 9 June 1923 Schomberg House, Pall Mall, London

Louise (Loosy) Duchess of Argyll
Born 18 March 1848
Married 1871 John Campbell Lord Lorne (1845-1914)
Duke and duchess of Argyll 1900
No children
Died 3 December 1939 Kensington Palace, London

Beatrice (Baby) Princess Heinrich of Battenberg
Born 14 April 1857
Married 1885 Heinrich (Henry or Liko) of Battenberg (1858-1896)
Four children: one girl and three boys
Died 26 October 1944 Brantridge Park, West Sussex

figures in their own time but are largely forgotten today. This book explores their personal stories, tinged with drama, tragedy, and scandal. Chapter 2 provides an overview and a brief pen picture of each of Victoria's daughters. Chapters 3 to 10 cover some key events in their lives in broadly chronological order, beginning with the grand dynastic marriage of Victoria (the eldest daughter) in 1858 (chapter 3) and finishing with the forty-year marathon of Beatrice (the youngest) censoring her mother's journal (or diary) after Queen Victoria's death in 1901 (chapter 10). The final chapter (chapter 11) gives glimpses of the next generation – Victoria's granddaughters.

1. Grand portrait of Victoria and her young family in 1846; her three eldest daughters to the right; her two eldest sons to the left.

Victoria had qualities that made her a great queen, but she was not at her best as a mother. It was a tragedy for her daughters that their father died so young, at the age of only forty-two. Albert was a good father, and the focal point of the family. The happiness Victoria found in family life was partly because this pleased Albert. For Victoria Albert always took first place, and their children came a poor second. Victoria was passionately devoted to her husband and perhaps she resented his time and attention their children took away from her. After his death she wallowed in her own grief and desolation and had little thought for her children or their loss. The fun of family life when Albert was alive was gone. Victoria became a stern and distant figure, and her children were always in awe of her even when grown up. Victoria's daughters were never allowed to forget she was their sovereign as well as their mother and her wishes should be obeyed.

2. Portrait of Victoria's four eldest daughters in 1849 – (from left to right) Alice, Victoria, little Louise and Helena. Beatrice is not yet born.

Victoria's daughters fell into pairs according to their age when Albert died. At twenty-one and eighteen the two eldest, Victoria and Alice, were considered grown up and their futures had been already determined by their father. These lay in arranged marriages to a foreign prince chosen to cement diplomatic relations. Victoria was married to the heir to the Prussian throne at the time Albert died, and Alice was engaged to the heir to another German state called Hesse-

3. Family photo at the time of Bertie's wedding in 1863 –
Louise kneeling on the left; Beatrice looking at a book with her mother;
Alice seated on the right; and Helena standing behind her.

Darmstadt. Politics and war would bring them great sadness and grave
disappointments. The middle daughters Helena and Louise, at fifteen
and thirteen, were still in the schoolroom. They lost the chance of a
great position in life that might have been arranged by Albert through
their marriages. Their husbands would be selected by Victoria and their
futures arranged to suit their mother. She turned her back on grand
foreign marriages and decided her younger daughters must remain
in Britain to support her. Things did not entirely turn out as Victoria
intended with shocks, scandal, and ructions in the family. The youngest
daughter Beatrice was only four years old when Albert died. She alone
of the daughters could have no memory of her father. Beatrice was
destined by Victoria for a life in her mother's shadow.

The name Victoria

The girl's name Victoria derives from the Latin word for victory (victoriam). It came into the royal family with Queen Victoria, born in 1819, who was christened Alexandrina (after her godfather Tsar Alexander II of Russia) and Victoria (for her mother Princess Victoire of Saxe-Coburg-Saalfeld). Before this the name was not used in the British royal family.

Victoria and Albert named their first daughter Victoria (shortened to Vicky within the family) and their first son Albert (shortened to Bertie) and expected these names to feature as frequently as possible among their descendants. There were six girls named Victoria in the generation of Queen Victoria's granddaughters and nicknames were needed to distinguish between them. Nicknames were very popular in the royal world since the same first names were used time and again.

Vicky's daughter Victoria was nicknamed Moretta and Helena's daughter was Thora. Beatrice's daughter was always Ena (another of her names). Bertie's daughter became Toria and Alfred's was Ducky (Alfred was Victoria's second son). Only Alice's eldest daughter, born at Windsor Castle with her grandmother present, was known by the unabbreviated name Victoria. In this book their nicknames are used to distinguish between the various princesses named Victoria; Alice's daughter is referred to by her full name of Victoria of Hesse-Darmstadt; Queen Victoria herself is always Victoria.

After Queen Victoria's death the name Victoria disappeared from the British royal family. George V's only daughter was called Mary (after her mother Queen Mary); Edward VIII had no children; George VI's two daughters were Elizabeth (Queen Elizabeth II named for her mother Queen Elizabeth the queen mother) and Margaret. Queen Elizabeth II named her only daughter Anne; King Charles III has two sons but no daughter; and the next heir to the throne, William Prince of Wales, has one daughter named Charlotte.

It remains to be seen whether the name Victoria will feature again in the future.

This is the fourth book in my series on *The Colourful Personal Life of Queen Victoria*. The first three books focus on the different phases of Victoria's life. *Young Victoria* is the story of her early years, including the difficult childhood that formed her resolute character and how she came to the throne as a teenager. *Victoria & Albert* looks at her marriage to Albert and how Victoria balanced the very different roles of sovereign and Victorian wife and mother. The third book, *Victoria, The Widowed Queen*, covers her long years alone as a widow after Albert's early death. This book takes on the story through the lives of Victoria's five daughters. Victoria herself remains a larger-than-life character in *Victoria's Daughters*. She was a controlling influence in her daughter's lives even after they were married. Her younger three daughters, in particular, never escaped their mother's orbit. When Victoria died in 1901 her surviving daughters fell in importance as members of the royal family and became more shadowy figures in the history books.

I chose to write the next in the series about Victoria's five daughters (rather than about her four sons who also had interesting lives) because of an imbalance in royal history. Princesses have been so often the forgotten heroines banished in marriage to a foreign land, usually as a teenager. Historically royal genealogy was traced through the male line and males took priority over females in the order of succession. Although Victoria's eldest child was a daughter all her four younger brothers ranked above her. This system, called male primogeniture, was only changed in Britain with effect from 28 October 2011. This means that Princess Charlotte of Wales born on 2 May 2015 (the daughter of William and Kate) keeps her place in the line of succession by order of birth and was not overtaken by her younger brother Louis, born on 23 April 2018. She is the first British princess to do so.

My books give a personal view of the story of Queen Victoria and her family, from many years of reading and research. They are not intended as a comprehensive account of her reign and times. This book focuses on how Victoria shaped the destinies of her daughters through their marriages; her domineering relationship with them; and how love, war, death, and disability shaped their personal lives. Charts and family trees at the back of the book explain the family relationships and the book is illustrated with portraits of Victoria and her family from my personal collection. It is almost half a century since I found the portrait of Queen Victoria in the attic that started this collection. She has never ceased to intrigue me.

4. Victoria with her family at her Diamond Jubilee in 1897. Her eldest daughter Victoria stands behind her mother on the left wearing a choker; Louise is two to the right of Vicky (next to her brother Bertie); Helena is far left in the back row; and Beatrice sits in a chair in the right foreground surrounded by her four children.

One reason Victoria is so fascinating is the wealth of original sources. Her voice comes down to us from history loud and clear. Victoria was a prolific writer who kept a daily journal (or diary) throughout her life and wrote thousands of letters to her daughters. Some of these have been published. Most notable is a multi-volume edition of edited extracts from the correspondence between Victoria and her eldest daughter, who became German empress (see the Selected bibliography under Fulford, Roger and Ramm, Agatha). For more than forty years, the two women wrote to eachother several times a week, exchanging family news and gossip and discussing state affairs. Equally enthralling is the online edition of Queen Victoria's journal published by the Royal Archives in 2012 to commemorate the Golden Jubilee of Queen Elizabeth II. I have drawn on these and other original sources to help tell the story of Victoria's daughters.

Royalty have always been the celebrities of their day and their personal stories from history can rival anything in *Hello* magazine. Read on to discover the story of Victoria's daughters – the bitter frustration of the eldest daughter as her life's ambition crumbles to ashes; the heroic death of the second in a deadly epidemic of disease; the battle of the third with ill health and drug dependency; the rumoured illegitimate baby of the fourth; and the determination of the youngest not to bend to her mother's will but to marry the man she loved.

2

THE FIVE DAUGHTERS OF QUEEN VICTORIA

Queen Victoria's first child was born at Buckingham Palace in London on 21 November 1840 just nine months and eleven days after her wedding to Prince Albert. The nation awaited the coming birth with great joy and some trepidation. That the baby would displace Victoria's hated uncle, Ernest Duke of Cumberland, as heir to the British throne was cause for celebration. But there was anxiety too over whether Victoria would come safely through the ordeal of childbirth. No one had forgotten the tragic example of Victoria's cousin Princess Charlotte, the darling of the nation, who died giving birth to a still-born son in 1817 aged twenty-one, after an agonising and mismanaged two-day labour. Charlotte was the only child of the prince regent (later George IV) and after him the next heir to the British throne. Had it not been for Charlotte's early death, Victoria would probably never have been born. (See chapter 2 of *Young Victoria: The Colourful Personal Life of Queen Victoria* for the story of *The Royal Race for the British Crown*.)

Victoria's labour began in the early hours of that Saturday morning, 21 November. As her labour progressed, the prime minister (who was

5. Victoria's sketch of her first daughter as a baby.

Sir Robert Peel), the archbishop of Canterbury, and other witnesses gathered in an adjacent room. The baby would be heir to the throne, so it was important that the birth be witnessed. This was to scotch any later suggestions of skulduggery or baby substitution. The practice of witnessing royal births began following the birth in 1688 of Prince James Francis Edward, the Stuart claimant to the British throne and better known to history as the Old Pretender. Despite the complete lack of any evidence, the Old Pretender was plagued by persistent rumours that he was not the son of James II and his second wife, Mary of Modena, but an unknown substitute baby smuggled into the palace in a warming pan (traditional type of hot water bottle). The practice of officially witnessing royal births was eventually abolished by George VI before the birth of his grandson Charles III in 1948.

The parents and the nation were all hoping that Victoria's first child would be a boy; the first male heir to be born to the reigning monarch for nearly eighty years. (The last, in 1762, was the future George IV, eldest son of Victoria's grandparents George III and Queen Charlotte). Just before two in the afternoon, when the baby arrived, the waiting witnesses heard the voice of the queen's gynaecologist, Sir Charles Locock, through the open door to her room. 'Oh Madam it is a princess'. 'Never mind' was her firm reply 'the next will be a Prince'[1]. Victoria was right, and the baby girl was followed within the year by a baby brother and over the following sixteen years by seven more babies, making a family of nine children in all – five girls and four boys. (Chart 1 has details of Victoria and Albert's nine children.)

The little girl born on 21 November 1840 was named Victoria Adelaide and created 'princess royal' by her mother. This is the title sometimes given to the eldest daughter of the reigning sovereign. Victoria and Albert soon recovered from any disappointment that their baby was not a boy. On the day she was born Albert wrote to his older brother in Germany saying that as 'Albert, father of a daughter, you will laugh at me'. Two days later he was already coming round. 'I should have preferred a boy, yet as it is, I thank heaven'[2]. The proud parents gave their little daughter the affectionate diminutive of Pussy, but later she became Vicky and so she would always remain within the family.

6. Vicky (left) completely overshadowed her little brother
Bertie Prince of Wales (on the right).

Vicky was a gifted child from babyhood, quick to learn, self-confident, and forward. She was the acknowledged leader of her siblings and shown off to visitors by her proud parents. In a way Vicky spoilt things for the younger children, none of whom could live up to her.

The Princess Royal of Great Britain

'Princess Royal' is a title that can be bestowed on the eldest daughter of the British sovereign as a mark of their high rank and prestige. The first princess royal was Princess Mary (1631-1660), eldest daughter of King Charles I, who was given the title at the suggestion of her mother. Queen Henrietta Maria was a French princess by birth and wanted to follow the custom at the French court where the eldest daughter of the king had the title of 'Madam Royale'.

The title of princess royal is given entirely at the sovereign's discretion and does not pass by right. There have been only six further holders of the title since the Stuart Princess Mary. The current princess royal is Princess Anne (born 1950), the only daughter of Queen Elizabeth II, who received the title from her mother in 1987. Princess Anne will hold the title for her lifetime notwithstanding that, since her mother's death on 8 September 2022, she is now the sister of the reigning sovereign (rather than the eldest daughter).

There can only be one princess royal at any time. Princess Anne was not eligible for the title during the lifetime of the previous princess royal, her great-aunt Princess Mary (1897-1965), only daughter of King George V. Princess Mary herself had to wait until the death of her predecessor who was Princess Louise (1867-1931) the eldest of the three daughters of King Edward VII. Queen Victoria was able to create her eldest daughter Vicky (1840-1901) the princess royal shortly after her birth because the title was then vacant. The previous princess royal, Princess Charlotte (1766-1828) eldest daughter of George III, had died several years earlier. Of the seven princess royals to date, Vicky was given the title at the youngest age and held it for longest (more than sixty years until her death in 1901).

As King Charles III has two sons but no daughter, it can be expected that the next princess royal will be his granddaughter Charlotte, the only daughter of William Prince of Wales and his wife Catherine. Princess Charlotte of Wales (born in 2015) will be eligible for the title in due course following the accession to the throne of her father and the death of Princess Anne.

Vicky completely overshadowed her brother Bertie (Albert Edward, Prince of Wales) who was born a year after her on 9 November 1841. His talents were modest in comparison, and he was always compared unfavourably to Vicky. When nine-year-old Bertie was informed that he was heir to the throne he was totally shocked since he had assumed that the much better-suited Vicky would follow their mother as queen. Bertie's innate good nature meant he bore his sister no grudge for his treatment as a child and remained fond of her throughout their lives. When Vicky was dying painfully from cancer at her home in Germany fifty years later, Bertie was there fighting her corner, trying to persuade the German doctors to give her bigger doses of morphine.

Albert was in thrall to his firstborn from the start and Vicky would always be his favourite child. When she married and left home at seventeen, he wrote to her that 'you can hardly know how dear you have always been to me and what a void you have left behind in my heart'[3]. Albert wanted an important future for his special child and thought he could achieve this through a great dynastic marriage to the future king of Prussia. He envisaged Vicky playing a leading role in European affairs as queen consort of a superpower. When he died unexpectedly in 1861, Vicky was twenty-one years old, living in Prussia, and expecting her third child. The German royal doctors forbade her from travelling to her father's deathbed, so Albert was denied the comfort of his daughter at

7. Caricature of Mrs Lilley, midwife to all of Victoria's nine children.

the end, and Vicky a last goodbye to her revered father. As we shall see in chapter 3, Albert's grand plans for his eldest daughter were not to be and Vicky's story is one of frustrated ambition and bitter disappointment. For all her father's intelligence and political acumen, she had also inherited some of her mother's worst character traits and could be obstinate, opinionated, and tactless. Vicky's greatest failure was her poor relationship with her eldest son.

Victoria's second daughter (and third child) was Alice Maud born on 25 April 1843. Like all her sisters and brothers, Alice was born at Buckingham Palace with the queen's gynaecologist Sir Charles Locock in attendance and under the care of her midwife and monthly nurse Mrs Lilley. It was always a sign that a new baby was imminent when an empty carriage left the royal mews for south London to fetch Mrs Lilley. Victoria dreaded her pregnancies and had a horror of what she called *the shadow side* of marriage[4]. She had great confidence in Mrs Lilley but was always pleased to see her go after 'lying in' (two or three weeks in

8. 'Prince Albert driving his favourites' (his wife and three eldest children) for an outing in Windsor Great Park.

bed following the birth) because this represented the end of her ordeal and the resumption of her normal life. Victoria was almost continually pregnant during the 1840s. Alice was born less than eighteen months after her older brother Bertie (born only twelve months after Vicky), and a younger brother Affie (Alfred) would arrive only fifteen months after Alice.

Alice is the baby in her mother's lap in the charming picture of royal family life shown in illustration 8. Albert understood the value of good public relations and was keen to promote images like this of the royal family with a happy family life. He is shown driving his wife and three young children for an airing in the park at Windsor Castle. By the mid-1840s Victoria's image was evolving from the fresh and innocent young queen, who represented a new beginning when she came to the throne as a teenager, to that of a respectable matron and mother of a young and wholesome royal family. The children were showcased on state occasions from a young age. The whole family are with Victoria and Albert (see illustration 9) to greet King Louis Phillipe of France on his arrival at Windsor Castle for a state visit to Britain in 1844. Alice is the toddler standing next to her sister Vicky. Even new-born Affie is on display lying in a nursemaid's arms.

As a child Alice was the peacemaker among her siblings and comforted Bertie when he bore the weight of their parents' criticism and was put in the shade by Vicky's brilliance. Alice would always be Bertie's favourite sister. On a rare occasion when Alice was punished by being sent to bed early with no supper, Bertie crept up to whisper to her through the door. Caught red-handed he explained that he only wanted to 'give Alee' (the children's nickname for Alice) 'a morsel of news'[5]. Alice was also close to her youngest brother Leopold (born in 1853) who suffered from haemophilia. His troubled childhood and adolescence were blighted by crippling bouts of the disease and tussles with his overprotective mother to achieve some form of independence. As a young adult Leopold found a haven in Alice's married home and was godfather to her second son (who also suffered from haemophilia).

The names of Victoria's daughters

Victoria's eldest daughter was named Victoria after her mother and Adelaide as a compliment to her godmother Queen Adelaide the widow of King William IV (Victoria's uncle and predecessor on the throne). William and Adelaide's two daughters, had they not died as babies, would have taken precedence over Victoria in the line of succession. Adelaide was always kind to her niece in childhood and Victoria was fond of her.

There was no track record in the royal family for the names of Alice Maud given to Victoria's second daughter. Victoria explained the choice in a letter to her uncle (King Leopold of the Belgians) as being old English names (Maud is a form of Matilda). Alice's biographer suggests that the choice of Alice is more likely to have been because Victoria's first prime minister and mentor, Lord Melbourne, had once told her he liked the name.

The third daughter received the names of Helena Augusta from her godmothers, Hélène of Orleans and Augusta of Cambridge. The duchess of Orleans was related to both Victoria and Albert by marriage. The duchess of Cambridge was Victoria's aunt, the wife of her father's younger brother Adolphus Duke of Cambridge.

Louise Caroline, the fourth daughter, was named as a tribute to two important figures in Albert's life – his mother Luise of Saxe-Coburg-Saalfeld and his step grandmother Caroline of Saxe-Gotha-Altenburg. Albert's mother disappeared from his life suddenly when he was five-years-old following a scandal about her love life. He never saw her again, but he did not forget her. After Luise's banishment her stepmother, Dowager Duchess Caroline, played an important role in the upbringing of Luise's two young sons – Albert and his older brother Ernst.

Victoria's last daughter was Beatrice Mary. No one has suggested a reason for the choice of Beatrice, so it seems her parents simply liked the name. The second name of Mary was in memory of Victoria's aunt, Mary Duchess of Gloucester, who died shortly after Beatrice's birth. Mary of Gloucester was the last surviving of the fifteen children of George III. Her namesake would be the last to die of Victoria's nine children.

Alice grew up to be most like her father in character; prone to overthink things and get depressed. She often looks melancholy or downcast in her portraits. Albert arranged another prestigious foreign marriage for his second daughter – not quite as dazzling as Vicky's but nevertheless important; and at eighteen Alice became engaged to the heir to the small German royal state of Hesse-Darmstadt. Effectively she was being sent to Germany to support Vicky in achieving her great destiny. As the eldest daughter at home when Albert died (Vicky was married and living in Prussia) Alice nursed her father and then took on the demanding role of caring for her distraught and hysterical mother. Victoria came to depend heavily on her daughter and would not later accept that, when Alice married, she could not be constantly at her mother's side. Chapter 4 relates how Victoria turned against Alice and a rift between mother and daughter developed. Sadly, they were never given the time fully to make it up. Like her father Albert, Alice died young and, by grim coincidence, on the anniversary of his passing.

9. Victoria and her children greet King Louis Philippe of France on his state visit to Britain.

As the 1840s went on, the babies kept on coming. Victoria and Albert had no idea how to avoid pregnancy and Victoria's repugnance of breast feeding meant she did not have this natural protection against ovulation. Their third daughter (and fifth child) was born on 25 May 1846 and named Helena Augusta. From babyhood she was always known in the family as Lenchen – an adaptation of Helenchen, the German diminutive for her name. Lenchen was the middle daughter

10. Portrait of Victoria's third daughter Lenchen in 1849.

and the middle child with two sisters and two brothers older than her and two sisters and two brothers who were younger. As a child Lenchen was a tomboy who preferred her brothers' games and enjoyed physical activities such as gardening, climbing trees, riding, and mucking out the stables. Such behaviour would doubtless have been considered unladylike in a princess and not encouraged. Lenchen retreated into conformity and became self-effacing, even-tempered, and compliant.

Victoria's daughters and haemophilia

Queen Victoria carried the defective gene for haemophilia and passed this on to her children. There is an ongoing debate about whether she inherited the defect from her mother, or whether it was a gene mutation in the queen herself. This debate is never likely to be settled with certainty. Haemophilia is a disorder of the blood whereby the factor that makes it clot is missing. Any bump or bruise can therefore cause a dangerous and potentially fatal attack of bleeding. Sufferers of haemophilia are almost always male, and they get it from their mothers. In modern times the disorder can be managed by drugs and blood transfusions. In Victoria's day there was no treatment. Boys who had haemophilia suffered terribly and most of them died young.

There is an element of lottery in how the defective gene is passed from generation to generation. Not all the sons of a carrier mother will necessarily suffer from the disorder, nor will all her daughters themselves be carriers. Victoria passed the haemophilia gene to one of her four sons (Leopold the youngest) and at least two of her five daughters (Alice and Beatrice) who in turn passed it on to their sons and daughters. There is a question mark over whether two more of Victoria's daughters also carried the gene – Lenchen because the death of her baby sons could conceivably have been due to haemophilia, and Louise because she had no children so her case cannot be known. Only the eldest daughter Vicky seems clearly free of the defect as there is no evidence of haemophilia in her eight children.

Through their marriages, Victoria's granddaughters took haemophilia into the Prussian, Russian and Spanish royal families with tragic consequences. Haemophilia was a known disease at that time, but the mechanics of how it was passed from generation to generation were not fully understood. If Victoria had known of the strong likelihood that her granddaughters would be carriers, would she have sanctioned the prestigious marriages that spread haemophilia into other royal families? There could be no way of knowing whether these young, eligible, beautiful, and apparently healthy princesses did or did not carry the defective gene. Until they gave birth to a haemophiliac son.

By adolescence Lenchen was chubby and deemed by her mother to be less good looking than her sisters. Victoria described her teenaged daughter as 'poor dear Lenchen, though most useful and active and clever and amiable, does not improve in looks and has great difficulties with her figure'[6].

Lenchen's childhood came to an end when her father died. At fifteen, she was considered old enough to take part in Albert's death bed ritual and was one of the group kneeling around his bed when the end came. Like all his daughters Lenchen worshipped her father and treasured the moments she spent with him. Had he lived she could have looked forward to some of her father's attention when, as the eldest daughter at home following Alice's marriage, Albert was planning Lenchen's marriage in turn and tutoring her for the role of wife of a foreign prince. Instead Lenchen was expected to sacrifice her matrimonial prospects to stay at home at her mother's beck and call. The widowed Victoria put her own comfort above her daughter's life chances. There would be no important foreign marriage for Lenchen. As shown in chapter 5, Victoria found an impoverished second son, a minor royal who agreed to live in Britain.

Lenchen complied with Victoria's wishes and looked for happiness in the unimportant marriage arranged by her mother. She acted as Victoria's secretary and carried out charity work, making a role for herself as patron of good causes and opener of events. In many ways Lenchen was the model for a modern-day princess. They are fewer biographies about Lenchen than any of her sisters, but she was a well-known royal figure in her day.

Victoria's fourth daughter Louise Caroline was born on 18 March 1848. Only three weeks after her birth, when Victoria had finished lying in, the whole family fled the threat of Chartist demonstrations in London to the greater security of Osborne House on the Isle of Wight. Louise was born in unsettled times and some biographers have drawn a parallel with her restless personality as an adult. Victoria later remembered 'all that eventful time when she was born, which timed with hourly news of revolution and civil war'[7]. 1848 was the year of civil unrest across Europe and several monarchs lost their thrones. The Chartist demands look modest today (for example a vote for every male over twenty-one, secret ballots, and payment of MPs) but were considered revolutionary at the time.

11. A popular print of the royal family around 1850:
Louise is the youngest child holding her sister's hand.

Louise, sometimes called Loosy by her siblings, was the most unconventional of Victoria's daughters. At thirteen when her father died, Louise was considered too young to attend his death-bed scene. When she was told Albert had died, Louise cried out in anguish 'Oh! Why did God not take me. I am so stupid and useless'[8]. Louise reacted very differently than her sister Lenchen to their dull and suffocating new life under Victoria's all-pervading gloom. Lenchen became self-effacing and bent to her mother's will; Louise was more rebellious. Victoria wrote to Vicky that Louise was 'dreadfully contradictory, very indiscreet and ... making mischief very frequently'[9].

12. Louise in 1856 with her younger brothers Arthur and Leopold.

All Victoria's daughters were taught to paint and draw as this was considered a necessary accomplishment for well-born ladies. But Louise had real artistic talent. She broke with convention and became the first British princess to go to school when Victoria allowed her to take classes at the National Art Training School and the Royal Academy. Victoria respected her daughter's talent and encouraged this. Louise became a sculptress – a highly unusual career for any woman at that time, let alone a princess. If you have been to Kensington Gardens in London, the statue outside Kensington Palace of the young Queen Victoria in coronation robes is by Princess Louise.

Louise was the most beautiful of Victoria's daughters but proved difficult to marry off. There are a lot of rumours about Louise and men, including that she had an illegitimate baby as a teenager (discussed in chapter 6). Like the grandmother for whom she was named (Albert's mother) Louise has a reputation tarnished with sexual scandal.

By the 1850s the pace of childbirth had slowed down for Victoria. She was thirty-seven when she gave birth to her fifth daughter, and ninth and last child, on 14 April 1857. Beatrice Mary, nicknamed Baby by her mother, was nine years younger than her next sister Louise and alone of Victoria's daughters had no sister to play with as a child. As their late baby, Beatrice was petted and indulged by her parents in a way that caused resentment among her siblings. Anecdotes in her father's lifetime show Beatrice as a cheeky toddler who basked in the role of youngest child. In one story she helps herself to more pudding after Victoria has told her 'Baby mustn't have that. It's not good for baby' saying 'But she likes it my dear'[10]. When Vicky's first daughter was born three-year-old Beatrice tried to avoid things she did not like on the grounds of being too busy as 'I must write letters to my niece'[11].

13. Baby Beatrice before her father's death.

Beatrice's life course was set on the night her father died when she was four years old. The first thing Victoria did, when she could be persuaded to leave her beloved husband's body, was to rush wildly up to the nursery and lift the sleeping Beatrice to put into her own bed, for comfort. During that desperate and sleepless first night, Victoria lay next to little Beatrice, clasping Albert's nightclothes; Alice was in a small bed next to her mother's. From that moment Beatrice rarely spent a night away from her mother for the rest of Victoria's life. She was one of the few who could lighten her widowed mother's gloom. But growing up at Victoria's side affected the little girl's personality and the confident toddler became a shy and reserved adult.

Beatrice was beginning a life in her mother's shadow. Victoria firmly intended that her youngest daughter would never marry but always stay a spinster as her companion. Any talk of suitors or marriage was banned in front of Beatrice. She seemed content to stay subservient to her mother until, at a family wedding, Beatrice fell in love. She was the only one of Victoria's daughters whose marriage was not arranged. Beatrice chose her own husband and fought for the right to marry him. Falling in love was Beatrice's one rebellion. She did not entirely win her battle and never escaped her mother's orbit. Beatrice's love story is in chapter 8.

Beatrice has a bad press with historians because she censored her mother's journals after Victoria's death. She destroyed her mother's original handwritten entries and only Beatrice's edited versions have survived (see chapter 10). But I think she may have been underestimated. For three decades Beatrice was at the right-hand and the mainstay of the most powerful woman in Europe – Queen Victoria.

Her three younger daughters were with Victoria when she died at Osborne House on the Isle of Wight on 22 January 1901. Alice had passed away more than twenty years before (chapter 7); Vicky was dying slowly and painfully in Germany (chapter 9). Lenchen, Louise and Beatrice lived to see Victoria's family torn apart and the world they had known change forever through the carnage of World War I. Vicky's son lost his throne when the German monarchy was overthrown and, for fear of losing his, Bertie's son George V was forced to abandon Alice's daughter, the tsarina of Russia, to a gruesome fate at the hands of the Bolsheviks. Lenchen died in 1923 aged seventy-seven and Louise at ninety-one in 1939. Beatrice was the last of Victoria's daughters and died at eighty-seven in 1944 during World War II.

3

IF THE PRINCESS
CAN LEAVE THE
ENGLISHWOMAN AT HOME

As the eldest daughter of the British sovereign, Vicky was an important asset in the royal marriage market. Her parents planned her marriage from an early age. Albert wanted a great future for his favourite child and thought he saw in Vicky the intellect and qualities to change the course of European history. Albert was German and, like many of his countrymen, dreamt of a single German nation united under a constitutional monarchy. There was bitter disappointment when the old order with its patchwork of small despotic royal states was reinstated after the Napoleonic Wars. Prussia was the strongest of these German states and, in Albert's mind, the natural leader of the German nation. In 1848 Prince Wilhelm of Prussia (next in line to the Prussian throne) fled to England as a refugee from revolution in Berlin (the capital of Prussia) and the two men became friends. Albert thought he could achieve his dream through marrying Vicky to Prince Wilhelm's only son.

14. As the eldest daughter of the British sovereign
Vicky was an important asset in the royal marriage market.

Vicky's intended husband was Prince Friedrich Wilhelm of Prussia
(1831-1888) known to his family as Fritz. They were first introduced
with marriage in mind when Vicky was ten and Fritz was nineteen.
This meeting was contrived when the Prussian royal family visited
London for *The Great Exhibition* of 1851. This magnificent showcase
for British products and industries was Albert's greatest achievement
and ensured his reputation for posterity. Fritz of Prussia was dazzled
by Vicky from the start. He was supposed to wait until she was grown
up, but he proposed in September 1855 when she was fourteen. While
the royal family were on holiday at Balmoral Castle in Scotland, Fritz

picked a sprig of white heather and gave it to Vicky saying he hoped she would agree to spend her life with him in Prussia. Victoria was so ecstatic you might have thought that it was Vicky's mother rather than Vicky herself who was to be the bride!

> I must write down at once what has happened – what I feel and how grateful I am to God for one of the happiest days of my life![1]

Vicky was still a child and surely too young to make a life choice, but she fell deeply in love with the bridegroom selected by her parents. The mutual devotion of Vicky and Fritz would not waiver despite all the trials that lay ahead.

Vicky and Fritz were married in the Chapel Royal, St James's Palace, London, on 25 January 1858 when she was seventeen. Illustration 15 shows them kneeling at the altar with Victoria, Albert, and their younger children on the right and Fritz's parents on the left. Victoria had poured scorn on the suggestion that the wedding of a future king of Prussia ought to take place in Berlin.

> ... the assumption of its being too much for a Prince Royal of Prussia to come over to marry the Princess Royal of Great Britain [in England] is too absurd, to say the least ... Whatever may be the usual practice of Prussian Princes it is not every day that one marries the eldest daughter of the Queen of England.[2]

As can be imagined, such high-handedness did not endear Vicky to her in-laws. She would always be an outsider to them, considered to be too English and not Prussian enough. During the years of her engagement, Albert tutored his daughter to play a leading role in European affairs. But Albert had sadly mistaken the situation in Prussia and saddled his beloved daughter with an impossible mission. Prussian princesses were expected to confine their interests to *Kinder, Küche, Kirche* (children, kitchen, and church) and not to meddle in state affairs. Vicky did not fit the mould and struggled to reconcile two conflicting demands – to fulfil her father's political dreams but to be a good Prussian wife to Fritz. She was not helped by a bombardment of letters from her mother lecturing her on appropriate behaviour for an English princess.

15. Vicky's marriage was the result of years of planning by her parents. Victoria and Albert stand on the right; Fritz's parents are on the left.

In 1862 Otto von Bismarck became first minister of Prussia. He recognised Vicky's talents and said she could be an asset to Prussia but only if she adapted to her new country.

You ask me what I think of the English marriage. I must separate the two words to give you my opinion. The 'English' in it does not please me, the 'marriage' may be quite good, for the Princess has the reputation of a lady of brain and heart. If the Princess can leave the Englishwoman at home and become a Prussian, then she may be a blessing to the country.[3]

But Vicky was not able to leave the Englishwoman behind. She never lost the unshakeable belief that everything in England was superior. The amenities of Prussian palaces were considered primitive compared to the comforts of her parents' homes; the dinner hour was unfashionably early; and she chafed at having to attend what she thought pointless social events organised by her mother-in-law. It was tragic for Vicky that her beloved father died so young. Albert would probably have recognised the shifting landscape and guided his daughter through the treacherous waters of life in Prussia. The adulation of her parents from babyhood had left Vicky with the firm conviction she was always right. She was the stronger character in her marriage and came to dominate Fritz who was more malleable and lacked confidence. As a result, Fritz and his English wife were marginalised by Bismarck and had little influence in Prussia.

Like her mother Victoria, Vicky fell pregnant quickly and her first child was born on 27 January 1859, just a year after her wedding. It was not always an advantage in childbirth to be a royal princess as doctors were afraid to intervene in case of blame if things went wrong. The German royal doctors had not examined Vicky, so it was not realised, until her labour began, that the baby was in the breach position. This was beyond the expertise of the royal doctors attending her and a specialist (a gynaecologist) was sent for. Due to a muddle however, the message was put in the post to him rather than delivered by hand. When the gynaecologist eventually arrived the following day, Vicky was in extremis. Recognising that immediate action was vital, he administered chloroform to the mother and wrenched the baby from the womb. Amazingly both survived. At first it was thought the baby was dead, until the midwife coaxed him into life. It was a boy and a future emperor of Germany. They called him Wilhelm soon shortened by his family to Willie.

What was not noticed for some time was that Willie's left arm was severely damaged during his traumatic birth. It would never grow to full size and could not be used normally. This was a severe blow; Prussian princes were expected to be full-bodied and excel at military pursuits.

Bismarck and the unification of Germany

In 1861 Vicky's father-in-law succeeded to the Prussian throne. Vicky and Fritz were now crown prince and princess of Prussia (next in line to inherit). The new King Wilhelm of Prussia (1797-1888) was an elderly man of conservative views who was soon on a collision course with his parliament. In 1862 he determined to lay down his crown rather than accept parliament's right to overthrow his plans for reorganising the army. This was Fritz's moment – a chance to take over from his father while he was still young (he was thirty) and steer Prussia and Germany towards the liberal, constitutional monarchy that he and Vicky believed in. But Fritz took fright and funked it. He persuaded his father not to abdicate and instead to appoint Otto von Bismarck (1815-1898) as first minister of Prussia. Over the following years Bismarck forged the unification of Germany through three swift wars in what became known as his policy of 'blood and iron'.

When Bismarck came to power, Germany was a confederation of nearly forty separate sovereign states the most important of which were Austria and Prussia. In 1864 Bismarck made an alliance with Austria to win the Second War of Schleswig-Holstein and eject Denmark from these two territories in north-west Germany. Three years later, in 1866, Bismarck turned on his previous ally, defeated Austria in a lightning campaign in the Seven Weeks' War, and annexed Schleswig and Holstein for Prussia. Other German states that had sided with Austria also lost their sovereignty and became part of Prussia. Prussia was now the dominant and by far the largest state in Germany, encompassing over sixty percent of both territory and population.

In a third swift war in 1870 Prussia defeated France in the Franco-Prussian War and the French provinces of Alsace and Lorraine were added to Prussian territory. King Wilhelm of Prussia was acclaimed as kaiser (or emperor) of a united German empire in the Hall of Mirrors at Versailles Palace near Paris in 1871. Fritz stood at his father's side during the ceremony. But Fritz's time had come and gone. Bismarck had ensured that the crown prince and his English wife were kept out of state affairs and had little influence over the future of Germany.

As a child Willie was subjected to (what we would regard as) cruel treatments to try to correct the damage. His right arm (the undamaged arm) was strapped to his side to force the toddler to use his left (the disabled arm). His left arm was plunged into the carcass of a freshly slaughtered hare, allegedly to transfer the life-force. When the little boy's neck became twisted and contorted (due to the weakness on his left side) the muscles were cut, and he was strapped into a straightening machine. It was all futile as the damage was irreparable. Vicky was ashamed of her son's disability and delayed showing him off to her parents, putting off their suggestions for a visit to meet their grandson. In the photo in illustration 16, Vicky holds up her son's left arm to disguise that it is shorter than the other and stunted. The little boy's balance was impaired, so he is leant back against the chair. As an adult Willie would also be at pains to disguise his disability. In portraits and photos, he is often shown with his left hand hidden in his pocket.

16. Vicky with her eldest son Willie; in this photo she tries to disguise his disability.

What was never understood is that Willie may have been starved of oxygen at birth and suffered some level of brain damage. Perhaps this partly accounts for his deeply unattractive and deluded personality as an adult. His difficult relationship with his mother must have also played a part.

Vicky's 'lost' sons

Vicky and Fritz had eight children, four of whom were sons (for a list of their children see chart 2). None of the boys would fulfil Vicky's longing for a son in the image of her beloved father, Prince Albert.

The eldest son Willie (Wilhelm born in 1859) had his mother's intelligence but there were grave flaws to his character perhaps exacerbated by the trauma of his birth and disability. Willie grew up with a hugely over-inflated idea of his own abilities and importance. He aped the Prussian militaristic style epitomised by his grandfather Kaiser Wilhelm I and was turned against his parents by the machinations of Bismarck.

The second son Heinrich (Henry) born in 1862 was more likeable but a weaker character. Henry was so often 'pig in the middle' between the two strong characters in his family – his mother Vicky and his elder brother Willie. The two were frequently at loggerheads and both expected Henry to be on their side. He seems to have dealt with this difficult situation by being easy going and trying to keep in with both sides of the family. Writing to her mother, Vicky recognised that Henry '... is always nice when he has been with us some time, but not when he has been set up by others [ie Bismarck and his elder brother Willie], and his head stuffed full of rubbish at Berlin'[4].

Sigi (Sigismund born 1864) died of meningitis in June 1866 at twenty-one months old. He was the first of Queen Victoria's grandchildren to die. Fritz was away with the army fighting in the Seven Weeks' War and Vicky was forced to endure her little son's agony on her own. She was consumed by grief and despair bewailing the loss of 'My little darling, graciously lent me for a short time to be my pride, my joy, my hope is gone – gone where my passionate devotion cannot follow, from where my love cannot recall him'[5].

Vicky focused all her hopes on her last son Waldemar (Waldie) born in 1868 '... my sweet Waldie, the dearest and nicest and most promising of my boys ... a fine, straightforward, noble, honest, courageous nature, ...so much more gifted than his brothers'[6]. But Waldie's life was also cruelly cut short. He died of diphtheria in March 1879, aged eleven, in the same epidemic that killed Vicky's sister Alice and her little daughter (see chapter 7).

17. Vicky with her teenaged son Willie;
he is already being turned against his parents by Bismarck.

Vicky loved her son (and Willie was an affectionate, happy, baby) but she could not come to terms with giving birth to a damaged child. She wanted her son to be perfect and in the image of her beloved father, Albert. As her own mother had done, Vicky constantly and fiercely criticised her children. Willie's ego was fragile, and he craved his mother's unconditional love. He did not get it and eventually he gave up trying to please her. Bismarck filled Willie's head with overinflated ideas of his own importance and abilities. The young prince turned his back on his liberal parents and modelled himself on his deeply conservative and autocratic grandfather, King Wilhelm of Prussia (from 1871 the German kaiser).

4

MORE A FUNERAL
THAN A WEDDING

A great burden fell on the shoulders of Victoria's second daughter Alice when Prince Albert became ill in November 1861. There were no hospital nurses at this time, and patients were looked after at home by their female relatives. As the eldest daughter living at home, this role fell to eighteen-year-old Alice. During the weeks she spent caring for her terminally ill father, Alice found a vocation for nursing. As a married woman she would become a pioneer of nursing in Germany and set up a training school for hospital nurses. She wrote to her friend Florence Nightingale that if she had remained single, nursing '... is the calling I should have most liked to follow'[1]. Alice was a calm and efficient presence in her father's sickroom (unlike Victoria, who was prone to emotional outbursts). When it all became too much for her, Alice retreated to her own room for a good cry but was soon back on duty with the same composed demeanour.

When Albert died on 14 December 1861, Alice took on the exhausting role of comforting her bereft mother. Victoria collapsed emotionally

18. Alice as the eldest daughter at home, before her father's death.

and gave way to extreme grief. Years later Alice would still remember those terrible first nights when she lay next to her sobbing mother until they both fell asleep from exhaustion in the early hours of the morning. She wore herself out to the point of collapse and had to be persuaded to go away for a few days for a brief respite.

Alice's fiancé Prince Ludwig (Louis) of Hesse-Darmstadt (1837-1892) feared she would back out of their engagement, but the wedding went ahead. The marriage had been arranged by Prince Albert before he died, and Albert's widow was determined to carry out his wishes. Alice and Louis were married six months after her father's death (on 1 July 1862) in the dining room of Osborne House on the Isle of Wight. What should have been a joyous occasion was completely overshadowed by mourning for the bride's father. The scaled down ceremony with a restricted guest list took place in the strict privacy of the queen's private home and was described by Victoria (in a letter to Vicky the following day) as 'more like a funeral than a wedding'[2]. Alice was permitted a white wedding dress but otherwise her mother insisted on a black trousseau.

19. More a funeral than a wedding –
Alice marries Louis in the dining room at Osborne House.

From the months they spent so closely together following Albert's death, Alice came to know her mother's character better than did any of her sisters. This later contributed to a breach between them. The trouble was that Alice could see through her mother to the underlying selfishness beneath. Once she found her feet as a married woman, Alice began to resist her mother demands, question the motives for her decisions, and even proffer advice. Victoria would not tolerate any lack of compliance to her wishes among her children and wrote to her uncle (King Leopold of the Belgians) that Alice was '... very unamiable and not changed to her advantage'[3].

One source of discord was Alice's inability to make the long and frequent visits back to Britain demanded by her mother. Victoria was firmly of the view that, despite her marriage to a foreign prince, Alice should continue to spend much of her time in Britain with her mother. She complained that Alice's mother-in-law (Princess Karl of Hesse-Darmstadt) was 'most unamiable ... about Alice's living a good deal here and about what is right and proper'[4]. Alice was on a lengthy visit to her mother when she gave birth to her first child at Windsor Castle on 5 April 1863. Victoria was present at the birth and the baby girl was named Victoria Alberta after both Alice's parents. (Chart 3 is a family tree for Alice and Louis's children.) Victoria simply would not understand that as wife of the future sovereign of Hesse-Darmstadt Alice had responsibilities in her new country. She saw no reason why her daughter's marriage should interfere with her own needs and the first years of Alice's married life were blighted by her mother's constant demands for long stays back in Britain.

Another area of friction was Alice's interest in gynaecology and female health. Victoria described this as 'indelicacy and coarseness' that Alice must have learnt from her in-laws since she was 'nice and refined' when she left home[5]. When Alice's younger sister Louise visited Darmstadt on her honeymoon tour, Victoria warned her against Alice's curiosity and shocking questions (probably about her periods and prospects of pregnancy). Alice and her mother also clashed over breast-feeding. Victoria had a repugnance for this natural function that she compared to 'our being more like a cow or a dog'[6]. When Alice persisted in breast-feeding her children against her mother's advice, Victoria named a cow in the royal diary 'Alice' after her daughter.

Living in Darmstadt (the capital of her husband's state of Hesse-Darmstadt) Alice experienced the horrors of being close to the front-

20. Alice – princess of Hesse-Darmstadt.

line during Bismarck's wars of German unification. She was heavily pregnant with her third child when the Seven Weeks' War between Prussia and Austria broke out in June 1866. Hesse-Darmstadt was allied to Austria and against Prussia. It must have been especially painful for Alice to be on the opposite side to her sister Vicky, the crown princess of Prussia. Alice sent her two young children (her daughters Victoria and Elizabeth) to their grandmother Queen Victoria in England for safety and, despite her advanced pregnancy, organised essential medical supplies and equipment for the army field hospitals. Austria was quickly defeated and when Alice gave birth in July the Prussians were occupying Darmstadt and she could hear the sound of gunfire.

The German royal state of Hesse-Darmstadt

Hesse-Darmstadt was one of the many small sovereign states that made up Germany before World War I. Its rulers had the title of 'Grand Duke' considered to be one up the royal ranks from mere 'Duke' and one down from 'King'. Only the largest of the German states such as Prussia and Bavaria were categorised as kingdoms.

When Alice married Louis in 1862, the grand duke of Hesse-Darmstadt was Ludwig III (1806-1877), her new husband's uncle. Ludwig III and his wife (a princess of Bavaria) were childless, and Louis was second in line to the throne after his father (Ludwig III's brother Karl). Louis's father died a few months before Ludwig III, so it was Louis who succeeded his uncle as Ludwig IV. Louis and Alice became grand duke and grand duchess of Hesse-Darmstadt in June 1877.

Although small in size, Hesse-Darmstadt had good connections with the European superpowers. Louis was married to the daughter of Queen Victoria; his aunt (Ludwig III's sister) was the wife of Tsar Alexander II of Russia. These links through marriage helped save Hesse-Darmstadt from the fate of other German states that sided with Austria and against Prussia in The Seven Weeks' War of 1866. Hesse-Kassel, where the ruling prince was a distant relative of Louis, and Hannover, where the king was a cousin of Alice, were annexed by Prussia and lost their sovereignty. Hesse-Darmstadt was lucky to lose only a chunk of territory.

But as the role of Prussia grew, the sovereignty of Hesse-Darmstadt and the surviving German states was eroded. When the German Empire was established after victory in the Franco-Prussian War of 1870, key functions such as foreign affairs and defence were taken away and centralised under Prussia.

The last grand duke of Hesse-Darmstadt was Alice and Louis's son, Ernst Ludwig (Ernie). He lost his throne, along with all the remaining sovereign princes, when the German monarchy fell in November 1918 at the end of World War I.

The baby was a third daughter whom she and Louis called Irene (the name means peace). Alice was soon in the thick of things again, visiting the hospitals and comforting the wounded.

Darmstadt was close to the fighting again when the Franco-Prussian War began in July 1870. Alice turned the palace into a Red Cross Depot and (although once more pregnant) wore herself out tending to the wounded and organising nurses and supplies. She wrote to her mother that 'so much rests on me and there are so many to help – the poor forsaken soldiers families among others! I have seen that all is ready to receive the wounded, and to send out help'[7]. At least this time the sisters were together and when Alice gave birth (to her fifth child) in October she was so weak that Vicky (whose own (seventh) child had been born a few months earlier in June) helped to breast feed the new born baby. How shocked their mother Victoria would have been had she known!

Alice's life in Darmstadt was not entirely happy. Her relationship with her mother deteriorated and she suffered a religious crisis. As the power of Prussia waxed through victory in Bismarck's wars so Hesse-Darmstadt fell in importance and Alice's role as its future grand duchess diminished. She became dissatisfied with her marriage and wrote her husband some hurtful letters setting out her feelings. She knew that Louis loved her, and he was a good husband and father, but he was not the soulmate Alice longed for.

There has never been any lack of love – only with time, the disillusion became hard to bear. I longed for a real companion, for apart from that life had nothing to offer me in Darmstadt. ... I have tried again and again to talk to you about more serious things, when I felt the need to do so – but we never meet each other – we have developed separately – away from each other; and that is why I feel that true companionship is an impossibility for us – because our thoughts will never meet.[8]

The most devastating blow for Alice and Louis was the death of their small son from haemophilia. The baby born in the war of 1870 had a pitifully short life. Like her mother Victoria, Alice was a carrier

of haemophilia. Alice's younger brother Leopold had the disease, so it was known to be in the family, but two-year-old little Frittie, short for Friedrich Wilhelm, was the first sufferer among Victoria's grandsons. Alice's letters home to her mother described Frittie's suffering and the agonising medical treatment when he had a dangerous attack of bleeding, lasting several days, from a small cut on his ear. Three months later, in May 1873, Frittie was playing with his older brother in their mother's bedroom one morning when he accidentally tumbled out of the open window. By evening Frittie was dead from an internal haemorrhage. Alice's brother Leopold, who was the little boy's godfather, tried to comfort his sister by suggesting that perhaps it was better Frittie had died young and been spared all the illness and pain of life as a haemophiliac. Alice was inconsolable, tormented by 'The horror of my Darling's sudden death'[9]. She never got over Frittie's death.

21. Alice's husband – Prince Ludwig (Louis) of Hesse-Darmstadt.

5

WHEN YOUR PARENT AND YOUR SOVEREIGN SETTLES A THING

After Albert's death, Victoria soon decided she must have the support of a grown-up daughter living with her as companion and secretary. As it became increasingly clear that the married Alice could not or would not fulfil the role, Victoria turned to Lenchen. She became distraught at the idea that this more compliant and self-effacing daughter might also marry a foreign prince and go to live abroad.

> A married daughter I MUST have living with me, and must not be left constantly to look about for help, and to have to make shift for the day, which is too dreadful! I intend (and she wishes it herself) to look out ... for a young, sensible Prince for Lenchen to marry, who can during my lifetime make my house his principal home. Lenchen is so useful, and her whole character so well adapted to live in the house, that (unless Alice lived constantly with me, which she won't) I could not give her up without sinking under the weight of my desolation.[1]

Victoria did not want to face the same tussle all over again, as she had with Alice, of competing for her daughter's attention. 'Lenchen could not and would not leave me, as in my terrible position I required one of my daughters to be always in England'[2]. She valued her own comfort above her daughter's future happiness. Victoria determined there could be no grand foreign marriage for Lenchen, as had been arranged by Albert for the two eldest girls. She would find Lenchen a poor prince who was content to live in Britain off his mother-in-law's money. To her mind 'plenty of good sense and high moral worth are the only necessary requisites. He need not belong to a reigning house'[3].

22. Lenchen was deemed by her mother
to be less good-looking than her sisters.

Her choice fell on Prince Christian of Schleswig-Holstein (1831-1917), the second son of a dispossessed German duke. Alice protested that the marriage was arranged to serve Victoria's needs rather than Lenchen's happiness, and this deepened the breach between them. Victoria viewed Alice's concern as unwarranted inference in her affairs and wrote angrily to Vicky.

> ... when your parent and your sovereign settles a thing for her good which interferes with none of your rights and comforts, opposition for mere selfish and personal objects – indeed out of jealously is monstrous. I cannot tell you what I have suffered.[4]
> She [Alice] has become so sharp and bitter, and no one wishes to have her in their house.[5]

Lenchen's prince was not very prepossessing. Illustration 23 shows her with Christian at the time of their engagement. Christian was fifteen years older but the bald, unattractive, man standing next to Lenchen in the photo looks more like her grandfather than her fiancé. Indeed, when he was invited to meet Victoria for vetting, Christian mistakenly assumed he was being considered as a husband for the widowed queen herself rather than for her daughter! Christian was not a handsome and dashing young prince; he was middle-aged, rather dull and plodding.

23. Christian was fifteen years older but looks more like Lenchen's grandfather.

Prince Christian of Schleswig-Holstein

Lenchen's husband is usually known as Prince Christian of Schleswig-Holstein. This was short for his full name of Schleswig-Holstein-Sonderburg-Augustenburg. He was the younger son of Duke Christian August of Schleswig-Holstein-Sonderburg-Augustenburg. Duke Christian August was a disappointed man, dispossessed of two claims to be a sovereign. He was a strong candidate for the throne of Denmark but was unpopular in that country and overlooked in favour of another German prince who became King Christian IX of Denmark in 1863. A few months earlier King Christian IX's eldest daughter Alexandra had married Queen Victoria's son Bertie.

Duke Christian August's second claim was to rule the duchies of Schleswig and Holstein as an independent state. This was also doomed to disappointment as mighty Prussia invaded and later annexed these territories in 1866. Duke Christian August was financially compensated but never truly gave up his claim and passed this to his elder son Friedrich.

Duke Christian August's two sons married into Queen Victoria's family. Friedrich married Adelheid of Hohenlohe-Langenburg, the daughter of Victoria's half-sister Feodora; Christian married Victoria's daughter Lenchen. Friedrich and Christian were friends of Vicky's husband Fritz, and this is how Christian's name came to Vicky's attention as a possible husband for her sister. Vicky was always on the lookout for suitable spouses for her sisters and brothers. Christian was vetted by Queen Victoria and introduced to Lenchen when they visited Germany in 1865 to unveil a statue of Albert in his childhood home at Coburg. The couple became engaged a few months later and married at Windsor Castle on 5 July 1866. The inter-relationship of the two families was further tightened when in 1881 Friedrich and Adelheid's daughter Auguste Viktoria married Vicky and Fritz's eldest son Willie.

In 1917, amid the carnage of World War I, George V changed his name (from Saxe-Coburg and Gotha) to the much more English sounding Windsor and dropped all other German names and titles from the British royal family. The newly widowed Princess Christian of Schleswig-Holstein (Sonderburg-Augustenburg) became known in her last years as simply Princess Christian.

In fifty years of marriage to Lenchen, Christian was never given any important royal role and appeared content to while away his time at his mother-in-law's court doing virtually nothing. In later life Christian was accidentally shot by his brother-in-law (Lenchen's younger brother Arthur Duke of Connaught) during a shooting party at Sandringham and lost one eye. He had a selection of false glass eyes for different occasions including a bloodshot version for when he had a hangover! Christian's party piece was to take out his glass eye and show it to guests around the dinner table.

Lenchen's engagement also aggravated an already deep political divide among Victoria's children caused by the thorny problem of who owned the duchies of Schleswig and Holstein in north-west Germany. These two disputed territories situated between Denmark and Germany were bitterly fought over in two wars in the mid-nineteenth century, during which they were lost by Denmark and invaded by Prussia. In 1866 (the year of Lenchen's marriage) they were annexed and became part of the kingdom of Prussia. With Vicky married to the heir to the Prussian throne, and Bertie to the Danish king's daughter, the loyalties of Victoria's children were split over the conflict. And it got even more complicated and divisive because Lenchen's fiancé was the brother of a third player in the drama, who claimed to rule the duchies as an independent principality. No wonder that Victoria had to ban any discussion of the issue on family occasions!

Despite the furore among the family over her engagement, Lenchen was content to accept her mother's choice. She and Christian were happily married for fifty-one years until his death in 1917. Victoria permitted them to have their own home so long as this was close to her and within her orbit. Christian was given the honorary position of Ranger of Windsor Great Park and their main home was at Cumberland Lodge in the park, near Windsor Castle. Lenchen and Christian had four children (chart 4 is a list) and lost two more sons as tiny babies – Harald at eight days old in 1876, and an unnamed still-born son the following year, 1877. The loss of these tiny babies is why there is a question mark over whether Lenchen, like her mother and her sisters Alice and Beatrice, was also a carrier of haemophilia. It is at least conceivable that their deaths were due to haemophilia. Lenchen's two surviving sons did not suffer from the disease. Neither of her two daughters had children of their own so it is impossible to determine whether they were carriers.

24. Prince and Princess Christian
of Schleswig-Holstein-Sonderburg-Augustenburg.

As Princess Christian of Schleswig-Holstein (her married title) Lenchen continued to serve as Victoria's secretary and undertook many public duties that her mother refused to do. Like her sister Alice in Germany, she was interested in nursing and strongly influenced by the work of Florence Nightingale. Lenchen's strengths lay more in persuading and organising than in hands-on nursing. She understood the pulling-power of royal patronage and was a formidable committee chairperson who was quite prepared to cut the discussion short and move on saying 'Then we all agree on that don't we?'[6]. During the Franco-Prussian War of 1870 Lenchen was head of the Red Cross

Ladies Committee and received an award for her work raising funds and sending supplies to both sides in the conflict. In 1887 she became first president of the newly founded Royal British Nurses Association and championed professional training and state registration for nurses. During the Boer War (1899-1902) Lenchen was instrumental in the purchase and equipping of *the Princess Christian Hospital Train*, sent to South Africa in sections and reassembled to treat the wounded. After her eldest son died of fever on active service during this war (Christian Victor 1867-1900) Lenchen opened a nursing home in Windsor in his memory.

Another of Lenchen's initiatives was the setting up of the Royal School of Needlework (RSN) in order (as she said) 'to restore the nearly lost art of ornamental needlework' and 'provide suitable employment for gentlewomen who, through loss of fortune or other reverses are obliged to earn their own livelihood'[7]. The written history of the RSN, published in 2022 to coincide with its one hundred and fiftieth anniversary, pays tribute to Lenchen as founder and first president. She was so much more than merely a name on the letterhead and led the fundraising and actively promoted the school across her fifty years as president. Quick thinking by Lenchen secured the reputation of the RSN for all time, when she accepted the commission to embroider Queen Victoria's funeral pall (the cloth covering the coffin). The time to complete the work was so short that no commercial studio would accept the commission. Lenchen said her school would do it. The work was completed in twenty-one hours of continuous stitching by a team of forty-five embroiderers working around the clock. You can see the exquisite, embroidered pall in photographs of Victoria's funeral on the internet. The RSN has subsequently undertaken many important royal commissions including for the coronations of Edward VII, George V, George VI, and Elizabeth II, and also the wedding dress of Catherine Princess of Wales. The approach whereby a number of stitchers work simultaneously on one piece using the same technique, so that it looks like the work of a single embroiderer, is still used by the school today.

Cousin Louie

Only one of Lenchen and Christian's children married and there were no grandchildren. In 1891 their second daughter Marie Louise (known in the family as Cousin Louie) married Prince Aribert of Anhalt. This was a small and unimportant sovereign duchy in the east of Germany. The marriage was a fiasco and possibly never consummated. Aribert was unkind to his wife and there is a story that Marie Louise found him in bed with a man.

In 1900 Marie Louise went on a trip to Canada to escape her awful situation. She was especially upset at the time by the death of her brother, Lenchen's eldest son Christian Victor (Christle), from fever on active service in South Africa during the Boer War. Christle was a favourite grandson of Victoria, and his death was a grievous blow to the frail and ailing queen in the last months of her life.

Marie Louise's incensed father-in-law, the duke of Anhalt, blamed her for the marriage breakdown. The duke annulled her marriage by royal decree (he had the right to do so under Anhalt law) and sent a telegram to Canada ordering her to return to Anhalt. Victoria rose magnificently to the occasion sending her own telegram to override that of the duke and say, 'Tell my granddaughter to come home to me'[8]. Although self-centred and overbearing Victoria could always be depended on in time of trouble. The list of accusation made against Marie Louise by Aribert was so dreadful the lawyers refused to read it to her. Even so, Marie Louise never accepted the annulment of her marriage and regarded herself as the wife of Aribert until he died.

So, Marie Louise came back to Britain where she was a fixture on the royal scene for the next sixty years. She developed into a colourful character who claimed to have tradesmen as well as princes among her friends. Pearly queens and kings turned out at her funeral. There is a story that Marie Louise took her own supply of gin and tonic into Westminster Abbey for the coronation of Queen Elizabeth II and emerged tipsy at the end of the service. Towards the end of her life Marie Louise wrote a marvellous biography called 'My Memories of Six Reigns'. Born in 1872 in the reign of Queen Victoria, she died in 1956 in that of Elizabeth II.

25. Princess Christian acted as her mother's secretary
and undertook many public duties that Victoria refused to do.

As a married woman Lenchen often suffered ill health and became
addicted to drugs. Popular over-the-counter remedies of the day,
such as laudanum, contained opium and morphine and were as easily
available as paracetamol or aspirin today. Lenchen was often laid low
by headaches, stomach pains, rheumatism, and eye problems. Her
mother considered Lenchen to be malingering and blamed Christian
for mollycoddling her. With robust health herself, Victoria was always
intolerant of illness in others. Even the royal doctor Sir James Reid
believed Lenchen to be suffering from hypochondria. He tried to wean
her off the drugs with some success.

There is speculation today that Lenchen might have suffered from another medical condition that stalked the royal family called porphyria, inherited from her great-grandfather George III. Porphyria is a chemical imbalance of the body, producing wide-ranging unpleasant and painful symptoms. The condition did resurface in some of Victoria's descendants. Vicky's eldest daughter and granddaughter were almost certainly sufferers.

Although she never knew it, Lenchen did have an illegitimate granddaughter. Valerie, born in 1900, was fathered by Lenchen's younger son Albert. Valerie was brought up in Germany by a Jewish family from birth and knew nothing about her natural parents. Until days before his death in 1931 Albert wrote to his daughter to tell her he was her father. This became important when Valerie later needed to prove to the Nazis that she was not Jewish. She appealed to her aunts, Marie Louise and her sister Thora (Helena Victoria) and they signed a statement to confirm her paternity.

6

SHE IS SO
VERY MUCH ADMIRED

There is a longstanding rumour that, when she was eighteen, Victoria's fourth daughter Louise had an illegitimate baby by a courtier. The case for this is based on the sudden dismissal by Victoria of her son Leopold's tutor after only a few months in post and the adoption of an unknown baby boy the following year by the son of Victoria's gynaecologist. The suggestion is that Victoria dismissed the tutor, called Walter Sterling, in August 1866 when she discovered his affair with Louise and turned to her trusted doctor Sir Charles Locock (present at the birth of all her own children) to help with the baby. Around the time of the adoption Sir Charles wrote a letter suggesting he was shielding a family secret and was not happy about this.

Henry Locock, as the baby became, told his own children before he died that he was the son of Princess Louise and had contact with his mother as a child. The Locock family have always believed this claim and his grandson appealed to the ecclesiastical courts for permission to exhume Henry's remains and take DNA to test if he was related to the

26. There is a longstanding rumour that
Louise had an illegitimate baby as a teenager.

British royal family. In 2004 this appeal was refused, and so Henry's assertion remains scientifically untested.

No firm evidence has ever emerged to substantiate these rumours about Louise. I would not find it surprising if she had fallen in love with a courtier. Victoria's unmarried daughters led exceptionally sheltered lives and had few opportunities to meet young men outside the court circle. Louise was devoted to her brother Leopold, and they were both clearly fond of Walter Sterling, also of his replacement the Reverend Robinson Duckworth whom some sources suggest was the courtier concerned. Perhaps Louise had a teenage crush on one of these young men. We know that her sister Lenchen had a crush on her mother's

German secretary (Carl Ruland also left Victoria's employment suddenly, in 1863). Nor was it unknown for unmarried princesses to get pregnant. It is widely believed that Princess Sophia, the unmarried fifth daughter of George III, gave birth to an illegitimate baby boy in 1800 who was brought up by his natural father. In Germany the teenaged Princess Marie of Mecklenburg-Strelitz, distantly related to Louise, was seduced (probably raped) by a footman and gave birth to an illegitimate child in 1897. Princesses were kept in ignorance of the facts of life until they married, and it is likely that the poor girl had no idea what the footman was doing or of the possible consequences.

But I do not find the case convincing that Louise did have a baby. Even with the voluminous skirts of the day it would have been hard to conceal a pregnancy in the late stages and there is no tell-tale missing period when Louise might have been away from court giving birth. The dates for the departure of Leopold's tutor Walter Sterling (August 1866) and the adoption of the Locock baby (December 1867) do not match up. Henry Locock's adoptive parents were just married when they got him as a baby and it seems at least as likely that they were the natural parents, Henry was born out of wedlock, and this was covered up. This could easily be what Sir Charles Locock meant when he wrote about unsettling events in his family. Sadly, stories handed down as family lore are not always accurate.

Louise was the most beautiful of Queen Victoria's daughters. Victoria was proud of her good looks, writing to Vicky that Louise 'is so handsome (she is so very much admired) and is so graceful and her manners so perfect in society, so quiet and ladylike'[1]. A female visitor to Osborne when Louise was twenty described her in glowing terms.

Tall and graceful in figure more than any other of the royal family, she is also far the most perfect in beauty – and, were she no princess, everyone would praise and delight in her noble, handsome face – so refined and well-proportioned in every feature.[2]

The royal portrait painter Sir Edwin Landseer went so far as to exclaim 'If I were a young man and a Prince I should never rest till that lovely girl had promised to marry me!'[3].

Despite such high praise, it was not an easy task for Victoria to find Louise a husband. She was more difficult to please than her sisters and rejected tentative approaches from the interested foreign princes. Louise was adamant that she could not marry anyone she did not like. Eventually Victoria decided to break with convention and look for a new son-in-law among the British aristocracy. But even here suitable and willing candidates were sparse; Louise was forced to compromise and accept someone she had previously rejected. In the end she married John Campbell Lord Lorne, a future duke of Argyll (1845-1914). She was the first British princess to marry outside the exclusive royal circle since Henry VIII's sister more than three hundred years before.

27. Louise's wedding at Windsor Castle in 1871.

John Campbell Lord Lorne

John Campbell (known as Ian) was the son of the eighth duke of Argyll. As the eldest son and heir to the dukedom he held the title marquess of (or lord) Lorne. Lorne was the grandson of Victoria's great friend Harriet Duchess of Sutherland and mixed in royal circles from childhood. When Victoria first saw him at two-years-old she described Lorne as 'a dear, white, fat, fair little fellow with reddish hair, but very delicate features'[4].

Victoria first approached the duke and duchess of Argyll about a possible match between her daughter and their son in summer 1869 when Louise was twenty-one. Lorne was intrigued by the idea, but his suit did not find favour. Louise felt under too much pressure and rejected him. A year later however when they were allowed to meet under more normal circumstances, they liked each other. Both were artistic (Lorne wrote poetry) and had similar interests. Lorne pressed his case, and this time Louise accepted him. They were married at St George's Chapel Windsor Castle on 21 March 1871. They made a handsome couple. Louise wore white satin with Honiton lace and her husband's wedding present – a diamond chain necklace holding a large sapphire. Lorne wore military uniform setting off his slim figure, long golden hair, and sparkling blue eyes.

In 1878 Lorne was appointed to the prestigious role of governor general (the sovereign's representative) in Canada. Louise accompanied him to Rideau Hall in Ottawa, the official governor's residence. To have the daughter of the British queen in Canada was a huge coup for the colony. Lake Louise in the Rockies was named after her, also the province of Alberta. Louise's first two names (Louise Caroline) had already been used in the United States of America (for Louisiana and North and South Carolina) so her third name was used for the Canadian province. But Louise soon returned to Europe and Lorne spent much of his tenure alone. Her lack of support was probably a reason when he resigned early in 1883.

In 1900 Lorne succeeded his father as ninth duke of Argyll and head of Clan Campbell. Since he and Louise had no children, he was followed as the tenth duke by his nephew.

Louise's engagement and marriage (like that of Lenchen) caused another upset in royal circles. For Vicky's Prussian parents-in-law (Kaiser Wilhelm I and his wife Augusta) it was unthinkable for Queen Victoria's daughter to marry someone not of equal royal blood. Even the usually affable Bertie was against the match, concerned that his sister might lose her royal privileges and that Lorne, as a commoner, would not fit into the royal family. Victoria's response to these objections shows her as more practical and in touch with the changing times.

That which you object to I *feel* certain will be *for* Louise's happiness and for the peace and quiet of the family ... Times have changed; great foreign alliances are looked on as causes of trouble and anxiety, and are of no good. What could be more painful than the position in which our family were placed during the wars with Denmark, and between Prussia and Austria? ... You may not be aware, as I am, with what *dislike* the marriages of Princesses of the Royal Family with small German Princes (German beggars as they most insultingly were called) were looked [on] ...[5]

The marriage of Louise and Lorne got off to a good start and both hoped for children. Over the years Louise took many cures at European health resorts but was always disappointed in her hopes of a pregnancy; possibly she had been made sterile by tubercular meningitis in childhood. Because there were no children we cannot know if Louise was a carrier of haemophilia. Their failure to have children took a toll on their relationship. The marriage became increasingly unhappy, and the couple mostly lived apart. At one time Louise seemed to loathe her husband. Perhaps it was dislike of living with Lorne that drove Louise away from Canada during his time there as governor general.

Since Louise was a member of the royal family, there was no question of divorce. In later years the couple grew closer again and Louise looked after Lorne in the last years of his life. It has been suggested that Lorne might have been homosexual, but no evidence has ever been found to support this. Princess Margaret is said to have repeated the story that Louise had to brick up the French windows in their apartment at Kensington Palace to prevent Lorne wandering out at night to seek assignations in Kensington Palace Gardens. In all likelihood this story is a falsehood. Lorne suffered from dementia and memory loss in old age. If he did wander at night, this is more probably the reason.

28. Princess Louise and her husband Lord Lorne.

Illustration 29 shows Louise at the height of her beauty. She kept her good looks and elegance into old age, working with a personal trainer on diet and exercise. Her childlessness was a tragedy for her. Louise loved children and was a popular aunt. She was an unfulfilled and restless personality who developed the reputation of a man-chaser. She was prone to create trouble in the royal household and did not always get on with her sisters! When her sister Beatrice's husband died Louise made trouble and must have deeply upset her sister by claiming her late husband had made a pass at her and loved her better than he did his wife. She was probably jealous of Beatrice's married life.

29. Louise was described as 'far the most perfect in beauty' of Victoria's daughters.

There are strong suggestions that Louise had a long and close relationship, possibly an affair, with her sculpture tutor, Sir Edgar Boehm. She was involved in a scandal when he died suddenly from a massive heart attack in 1890. Louise was alone with Boehm in his studio at the time and rumour has it that they were making love. Louise initially tried to deny she was there at all. The story she eventually told her mother, that Victoria accepted, was that Boehm had been moving a heavy piece of sculpture and collapsed.

7

THIS DEAR, TENDER-HEARTED, NOBLE-MINDED, SWEET CHILD

Alice was the first of Queen Victoria's children to die, aged only thirty-five. Illustration 30 is a portrait of Alice not long before her death. On 8 November 1878, Alice sent her mother a telegram from Darmstadt to say that her eldest daughter Victoria of Hesse-Darmstadt had caught diphtheria. An epidemic of this highly infectious and deadly disease was raging in Germany, and it now swept through the palace in Darmstadt. One by one the other children succumbed, except the second daughter Ella (short for Elisabeth) who was hurried off to stay with her German grandmother. Then Louis too fell ill. Alice nursed them all herself, but she could not save her youngest child. She wrote to her mother.

> With a heart rung with pain and fear I write a few lines. ... and my sweet little May so bad – so bad; will she get through it! My little one – my last! Oh it is agony! ... Husband and four children between life and death ...[1]

30. Alice was the first of
Victoria's children to die.

On 16 November, the diphtheria membrane closed across the throat of Alice's four-year-old daughter May (short for Marie) and the little girl choked to death.

Alice is said to have caught diphtheria from comforting her son Ernie (Ernst Ludwig) over his little sister's death. She was an experienced nurse and knew about the need for infection control and social distancing. But Ernie had developed a morbid fear of death after his brother Frittie's accident (see chapter 4). When she had to tell him about May, Alice gave her son a hug. In announcing the sad news of Alice's death to the British parliament, Victoria's prime minister Benjamin Disraeli famously called this moment *a kiss of death*.

> My Lords, there is something wonderfully piteous in the immediate cause of her death. The physicians who permitted her to watch over her family enjoined her under no circumstances whatever to be tempted into an embrace. Her admirable self-restraint guarded her through the crises of this terrible complaint in safety. ... But it became her lot to break to her son, quite a youth, the death of his youngest sister, to whom he was devotedly attached. The boy was so overcome with misery that the agitated mother to console him clasped him in her arms – and thus received a kiss of death.[2]

Exhausted and at a low ebb, Alice was not strong enough to throw off the disease; perhaps like her father she did not have the will to fight for life. Alice died on 14 December 1878 – seventeen years to the day since her father's death. Her last reported words were 'Dear Papa ...'[3].

For Victoria the differences between mother and daughter were instantly forgotten as she remembered only Alice's loving care in the dark days of Albert's death.

That this dear, talented, distinguished, tender hearted, noble minded, sweet child, who behaved so admirably, during her dear Father's illness, & afterwards, in supporting me, & helping me in every possible way, – should be called back to her Father, on this very anniversary, seems almost incredible, & most mysterious![4]

Alice's death left behind her widower Louis and five surviving children aged between six and fifteen – their daughters Victoria, Ella, Irene, and Alix, and their son Ernie. Victoria took a special interest in these motherless grandchildren receiving regular reports from Darmstadt and having them stay with her as much as possible. She was a better grandmother than she had been a mother.

In Britain the story of Princess Alice's early death, devotedly nursing her family through a dangerous epidemic, captured the public imagination and made her a Victorian heroine. With our recent experience of covid-19, it still resonates with us today. My collection of portraits of Queen Victoria and her family includes a commemorative print from the time of Alice's death that depicts the deadly moment when she embraced her son. Found in a junkshop, this was clearly once a treasured possession as it is framed in an elaborate carved wooden frame with five panels. The central panel is a portrait of Alice; in four side panels she is shown tending the sickbeds of her family. In one she kisses Ernie and is infected with the disease. Unfortunately, this print is too fragile to take out of the frame and photograph for this book.

The tragic story of Alice's family

Alice and Louis had seven children (chart 3). The story of this branch of Victoria's family is as dramatic as any thriller novel or television soap opera. Haemophilia took a toll among Alice's children and grandchildren. Her second son Frittie (Friedrich Wilhelm) died at two-years-old from haemophilia in 1873; her daughters Irene and Alix were carriers and took haemophilia into the Prussian and Russian royal families. Irene married her cousin Heinrich, the second son of Vicky and Fritz. They had three sons, two of whom were haemophiliacs. Alix married Tsar Nikolai II of Russia (Nicky) and their only son suffered from haemophilia. Only two of Alice's children were clearly free of the disease – her eldest daughter Victoria of Hesse-Darmstadt and her elder son Ernie.

Victoria warned her granddaughters against marrying into Russia and she was right. Thousands were trampled to death at Nicky and Alix's coronation and they, with their five children, were butchered by Bolsheviks in 1918 during the Russian revolution. Alix's sister Ella met a similar fate at the hands of the Bolsheviks. They were not the last of Alice's descendants to die by violence. Her grandson Earl Mountbatten of Burma was murdered, with other members of his family, on a fishing trip in 1979, when their boat was blown up by the Irish Republican Army (IRA). Lord Mountbatten was the son of Alice's eldest daughter Victoria of Hesse-Darmstadt.

Alice's son Ernie became grand duke of Hesse-Darmstadt on the death of his father in 1892. Ernie's marriage to his cousin Victoria (Ducky), the daughter of Queen Victoria's second son, was a total failure and they divorced in 1901. Their only child Elisabeth died of typhoid in 1903 at eight-years-old, while on a trip with her father to Nicky and Alix at their hunting lodge in Poland. Ernie found happiness in a second marriage but only weeks after his death in 1937 tragedy struck again. Ernie's son Georg Donatus and his wife Cecile with their two small children and Ernie's widow were wiped out in a plane crash. They were on the way to the wedding of Ernie's younger son in London. Cecile was heavily pregnant, and another baby was born and died during the accident. Cecile was the sister of Philip Duke of Edinburgh.

8

I HOPE AND PRAY THERE MAY BE NO RESULTS!

After Alice's death in 1878, Victoria toyed briefly with the idea of marrying Beatrice to Alice's widower Louis, Grand Duke Ludwig of Hesse-Darmstadt. This was to provide her five motherless Hesse-Darmstadt grandchildren, of whom she was very fond, with a new mother. Probably it was only a fleeting thought as from early childhood Beatrice was earmarked as the daughter who would stay at home with her mother. Nevertheless, Victoria was much annoyed to be told that any such plan would not get off the ground as it was against the law in Britain at that time to marry the widower of a deceased sister (the law was changed in 1907). She never could tolerate being thwarted.

Illustration 31 shows Victoria with her youngest daughter in 1871, when Beatrice was fourteen. She seemed to accept her destiny as her mother's companion, but to be on the safe side Victoria banned any discussion of love or marriage in front of Beatrice. The illustration sums up their relationship as Victoria saw it. Beatrice is depicted as the devoted daughter, clinging to and subservient to her mother; Victoria

31. Beatrice as a teenager, already the close companion of her mother.

is more confident, pleased to be the centre of her daughter's attention. But there will eventually be an upset when Beatrice meets her prince.

In 1884 Beatrice and her mother travelled to Alice's old home in Darmstadt for the wedding of Alice's eldest daughter and Victoria's favourite granddaughter, Victoria of Hesse-Darmstadt. Victoria had been present at this granddaughter's birth in Windsor Castle in the days when she and Alice were still close. Victoria of Hesse-Darmstadt was marrying Prince Ludwig (Louis) of Battenberg, eldest of the four handsome and dashing Battenberg brothers. The brothers were closely related to the Hesse-Darmstadt royal family (they were first cousins of Alice's husband Louis) but not top-drawer royalty because their father had married outside the exclusive royal circle (to a mere countess). To her credit Victoria was not in the slightest bothered by the bridegroom's lessor royal status. She was always keen to welcome 'new blood' into her family and very much approved her favourite granddaughter's choice. This was in stark contrast to the attitude in Prussia where Vicky's father-in-law, Kaiser Wilhelm I, absolutely forbade the marriage of Vicky's daughter to Louis of Battenberg's younger brother.

With the support of Alice, Louis of Battenberg, although a German prince, had joined the British navy at the age of fourteen. He would rise to be First Sea Lord (professional head of the Royal Navy) before being forced to resign at the start of World War I because of his strong German connections. He and his wife Victoria of Hesse-Darmstadt were the parents of Earl Louis Mountbatten of Burma and the grandparents of Prince Philip Duke of Edinburgh, consort of Queen Elizabeth II.

A great crowd of royalty from around Europe descended on Darmstadt for the royal wedding in 1884; Victoria called them 'the royal mob'. Behind the scenes at what should have been a happy occasion, emotions were seething. Victoria was deeply upset over the recent engagement of the bride's sister Ella (Alice's second daughter, Elisabeth) to Grand Duke Serge of Russia. Victoria was an inveterate matchmaker for her grandchildren, but she did not approve of marriages into the Russian royal family. She regarded Russia as a barbarous and untrustworthy country. Then it was revealed that on the same day as his daughter's wedding, Alice's widower Louis had secretly married his mistress (called Alexandrine de Kolemine). His daughters liked her and felt it was a good idea for their father to have someone to care for him after they were married. But when Victoria found out the following day, she was furious that her son-in-law had, as she saw it, dishonoured Alice's memory. She insisted the marriage be annulled and, amazingly, she got her way. Louis knuckled under and his all-too-brief wife was paid to go away.

But what caused the most tension at the Darmstadt wedding was the obvious and growing attraction between Beatrice and the bridegroom's younger brother Heinrich (Henry) of Battenberg (1858-1896) known by his nickname of Liko.

Saint Elisabeth of Russia (1864-1918)

One of Victoria's granddaughters is a canonised saint of the Russian Orthodox Church. Alice's second daughter, Elisabeth of Hesse-Darmstadt (called Ella in the family), was considered the most beautiful princess of her generation and a great catch on the royal marriage market. Ella rejected a proposal from her cousin Willie (Vicky's son), the future Kaiser Wilhelm II, before accepting Grand Duke Serge of Russia. Serge was another cousin she had known from childhood – his mother Tsarina Marie Alexandrovna was a princess of Hesse-Darmstadt and Ella's great-aunt.

Victoria did not want to see any of her granddaughters married into the Russian royal family. She did her best to dissuade her granddaughter, but Ella married Serge in 1884. Victoria was right to be concerned. Serge was a difficult young man who was not altogether liked in the family. He was seen to be controlling in his relationship with Ella and thought possibly to be a repressed homosexual. The couple had no children. Ella turned to religion; in 1891 she converted from the Lutheran faith of her birth to Russian Orthodoxy, the religion of her new country.

Serge was an unpopular governor of Moscow; in 1905 he was assassinated by a terrorist bomb during civil unrest. Ella heard the explosion and rushed out to help pick up her husband's shattered remains from the snow. She visited the assassin in prison and forgave him. After Serge's death she became a nun, and set up a convent in Moscow working with the poor and sick.

In 1918, following the Russian revolution and the abolition of the monarchy, Ella was arrested with her devoted companion Sister Varvara (Barbara). They were butchered by the Bolsheviks a day after the brutal murder of the ex-tsar and tsarina (Ella's sister) and their five children. Together with other members of the Russian royal family, Ella and Varvara were thrown alive down a mine shaft followed by hand grenades and left to die. Their remains were rescued during the Russian Civil War and sent east first to Beijing, China and then to Jerusalem where Ella and Varvara are buried in the garden of Gethsemane. Ella was canonised by the Russian Orthodox Church in 1981 (the church outside Russia) and 1992 (in Moscow).

When Beatrice said she was in love and wanted to marry Liko, Victoria was appalled. She refused to countenance the idea and employed a weapon of silence to try to bring her daughter to heel. For months she would not speak to Beatrice, and they communicated by notes pushed across the breakfast table. But Beatrice was equally resolute and did not give way. Faced with this determination Victoria was forced to accept the inevitable and call a truce. She agreed to the marriage but on her own terms. Liko must resign his commission in the Prussian army and the couple would live with her and not have a home of their own.

As the wedding day approached Victoria was tortured by the horrifying thought of Beatrice's wedding night. She had enjoyed her own sexual relationship with Albert but could not bear the thought of her treasured youngest daughter in the marriage bed.

> I count the months, weeks and days that she is still my own sweet, unspoilt, innocent lily and child. That thought – that agonising thought which I always felt, and which I often wonder any mother can bear of giving up your own child, from whom all has been so carefully kept and guarded – to a stranger to do unto her as he likes is to me the most torturing thought in the world. While I feel no girl could go to the altar (and would probably refuse) if she knew all, there is something very dreadful in the thought of the sort of trap she is being led into.[1]
>
> I hope and pray there may be no *results*![2] [By 'results' she means children.]

Beatrice and Liko were married in the village church at Whippingham, near Osborne House on the Isle of Wight on 23 July 1885. This was the greatest day in the history of the Isle of Wight. The small parish church of St Mildred's was quite unsuited to a great royal occasion, but Beatrice loved Osborne above all her mother's homes. Even with additional seating erected in the churchyard there were many who might have hoped to be on the guest list and were disappointed. Victoria was gleeful not to invite her ex-prime minister William Gladstone whom she loathed. He had just left his second (of four) term of office. The bride was walked up the aisle by her mother and her eldest brother Bertie, Prince of Wales. As Victoria's favourite daughter Beatrice wore her mother's wedding veil of Honiton lace; none of her sisters had been afforded this privilege. Liko looked imposing in the white uniform of his elite Prussian regiment so that Bertie's wife called him 'Beatrice's Lohengrin' (the swan knight of German legend).

32. Beatrice's wedding in Whippingham Church in 1885.

Victoria lost her fight to prevent Beatrice marrying but the wedding heralded in some of the happiest years of her life. She enjoyed having a handsome young man about the house again and became very fond of this son-in-law. Liko got on so well with his mother-in-law that he was even able to persuade her to relax the rules banning smoking in her homes. Victoria abhorred smoking and had banished Lenchen's husband Christian (an inveterate smoker) to a room outside in the yard if he must indulge in the obnoxious habit. Victoria was mellowing in her old age. She called Liko 'a bright sunbeam in my Home'[3].

33. Victoria with her youngest grandchild –
Maurice of Battenberg born in 1891.

There were results – Beatrice and Liko had four children (a girl and three boys) whose presence enlivened Victoria's homes (see chart 5). Her pleasure in being a grandmother is clearly shown in the photo of Victoria with Beatrice's youngest son Maurice, born in 1891, the last of her forty grandchildren (illustration 33). She looks like any doting grandmother. Maurice was one of that generation of young men slaughtered in World War I. He was killed on the Western Front in October 1914.

After her marriage, Beatrice continued in the role of Victoria's carer and personal assistant. But as the years went by Liko became less content with staid married life at his mother-in-law's side.

Liko's father (Prince Alexander of Hesse-Darmstadt) had been a career soldier decorated for valour on the field of battle by four countries (Austria, Prussia, Hesse-Kassel, Russia); his brother Louis (married to Victoria of Hesse-Darmstadt) was a rising star in the British navy; another brother had been elected sovereign ruler of Bulgaria. Liko craved his own adventure. In 1895, after ten years of marriage, he persuaded Victoria to let him take part in a military expedition to the Ashanti region of West Africa (now part of Ghana). Victoria understood the danger and the risk of disease and was against his going from the

34. Prince and Princess Henry of Battenberg.

start. But Liko pleaded that he wanted to do something to serve his adopted country; Beatrice supported her husband; and Victoria was caught in a trap because she had already given permission for her grandson Christle (Lenchen's eldest son Christian Victor) to go.

Liko caught malaria shortly after he arrived in West Africa and died on 20 January 1896 on board the ship bringing him back to England. He was thirty-seven years old; Beatrice a widow at thirty-eight (four years younger than her mother when widowed). Beatrice went away with her children for a month to mourn her husband before returning to Victoria's side. This was the only significant time Beatrice ever spent apart from her mother until Victoria died.

Liko's last journey

Liko said goodbye to his mother-in-law at Windsor Castle on 6 December 1895 and left to join the British military expedition to Ashanti the following day. The expedition was one of a series despatched by the British government to subdue the Ashanti empire and protect British trading interests. Despite earlier undertakings the Ashanti King Prempeh was continuing to raid neighbouring territories and sell the inhabitants into slavery.

The British force landed at Cape Coast in West Africa and on 27 December began the march north to Kumasi, capital of the Ashanti region. The campaign would be over by early February without a shot being fired. King Prempeh was deposed and sent into exile. But the toll of disease on the British troops was great. Liko became ill with malaria on 10 January 1896 during the march north and was sent back to the coast to recover.

At first the prognostication was good but then his condition worsened, and despite Liko's protests it was decided to send him home on the warship HMS Blonde.

Liko died at sea off the coast of Sierra Leone on 20 January 1896. He felt the sadness of dying alone away from his family and left messages to be delivered later to his wife. When she received the news of his death by telegram on 22 January Beatrice was totally stunned and could say only 'The life has gone out of me'[4]. The crew of the Blonde were faced with a problem – how to ensure the prince's body reached Britain in reasonable shape despite the heat of the tropics. They were forced to improvise by making a waterproof coffin out of old biscuit tins and pickling the corpse with rum.

At Madeira Liko's remains were transferred to HMS Blenheim for the rest of the journey back to Britain. He had asked to be buried in Whippingham church where he and Beatrice were married. On 4 February 1896 the coffin was met at Portsmouth by Beatrice with Bertie and Liko's brothers and taken across the Solent in the royal yacht Alberta. At Cowes Victoria and Liko's children were waiting on the quay. The funeral service was held the following day. Liko rests in the Battenberg chapel in Whippingham church. Forty-eight years later his widow Beatrice joined him.

9

THE TRAGEDY
FOR MY POOR CHILD
IS TOO GHASTLY

As Beatrice's married life was beginning, Vicky's was coming to an end. When Albert arranged her marriage to Fritz, he envisaged them ruling a united Germany as a liberal, constitutional monarchy. These dreams had come to dust. In thirty years of waiting for the throne, Fritz had been cast aside by Bismarck in favour of his eldest son, Willie. Prussia was an absolute monarchy, set on the militaristic path that led to two world wars.

Fritz's father, Kaiser Wilhelm I, lived to the exceptionally old age (for those times) of ninety. By 1888 he was near the end, but the tragedy was that Fritz was also a dying man. The year before, a growth had appeared in Fritz's throat and the German doctors diagnosed cancer of the larynx. They recommended an operation to remove the larynx and save his life. Vicky fought against her husband's diagnosis, initially keeping it secret from Fritz and favouring the view of an English specialist, Morrell Mackenzie, who was called in for a second opinion. Mackenzie thought the growth was benign and that an operation was not necessary. A bitter tussle ensued. Victoria warned her daughter not to rely too heavily on the favourable diagnosis, but Vicky would not listen. She was a spiky character who had never fitted in in Prussia; her high-handed behaviour now made her even more unpopular. She was calumnied in Germany for her relentless cheerfulness and refusal to accept the seriousness of her husband's illness. But who can really blame her? Vicky was losing her beloved husband and her life's purpose and ambition were crumbling away.

35. Vicky's beloved husband Fritz as Kaiser Friedrich III; he was already a dying man.

The German doctors were right, it was cancer. No-one could know who would die first – the frail father or his desperately ill son. When Kaiser Wilhelm I died in March 1888, Vicky and Fritz were in Italy, over-wintering for his health to escape the harsh Prussian weather. The cancer was so advanced that Fritz could no longer speak and had to breathe through a canula (tube) inserted in his throat. His first action on hearing he was now Kaiser Friedrich III was to invest Vicky with the Order of the Black Eagle (the highest decoration he could bestow). He wrote down his thanks to his doctor (as he could no longer speak) saying 'I thank you for having made me live long enough to recompense the valiant courage of my wife'[1].

Vicky and Fritz returned to Germany and to the Neues Palais (New Palace) at Potsdam near Berlin where Fritz had been born, and where he had now decided to die. The new kaiser was too ill to make any of the changes he and Vicky had planned and was forced to accept the hated Bismarck as his prime minister. Victoria made a last visit to Prussia to say goodbye to her best-loved son-in-law and show solidarity with her daughter Vicky. Fritz died at the Neues Palais on the morning of 15 June 1888 after a reign of just ninety-nine days. Vicky was a widow at forty-seven with no future role to play.

36. Queen Victoria arrives in Berlin to say goodbye
to her best-loved son-in-law.

Vicky's son Willie, now the new Kaiser Wilhelm II, behaved appallingly. Bismarck had destroyed Vicky's reputation as an English spy and a bad influence on Fritz. He had done his best to turn Willie against her and Vicky had long since ceased to have any influence over her eldest son. The moment his father died; Willie had the Neues Palais cordoned off with troops to prevent (he said) his mother sending state documents to England. He virtually accused his parents of treason. When Vicky came out into the garden to pick roses for her husband's deathbed, she was roughly ordered back inside. The widowed Vicky was subjected to a smear campaign with accusations she had dominated her husband, mismanaged his illness, and betrayed Germany. Her reputation would not be rehabilitated in Germany until the second half of the twentieth century.

1888 is known in Germany as *The Year of the Three Kaisers* – Wilhelm I, Friedrich III, and Wilhelm II. From the start however, Wilhelm II made it clear that he regarded himself as the successor of his grandfather rather than of his father. Fritz was soon forgotten in the excitement of the new reign – no more than a footnote to history. Vicky wrote bitterly to her mother that 'Wilhelm II succeeds Wilhelm I ... the sooner he (Fritz) is forgotten the better, therefore the sooner his widow disappears the better also'[2].

Victoria sympathised with her daughter deeply. Twenty years before, when Vicky's son Sigismund had died from meningitis as a toddler, Victoria had pulled up her daughter sharply for over-dramatizing her grief. In Victoria's mind no grief could possibly equal her own.

> But it is not right in you, dear child, to say you would give up everything, 'home, them all' to get little Siggi back. That is really wrong dearest child! It is tempting providence. Think what is a child in comparison with a husband.[3]

But now she understood her daughter's dreadful plight 'The tragedy for my poor child is too ghastly much worse even than mine in 1861'[4].

Vainglorious, pompous, deluded, Willie believed he was ordained by God to rule and referred to himself as the *All-Highest*. He liked to portray himself (see illustration 38) as a great military leader, but he was essentially a weak man who never saw any military action.

Willie was soon champing at Bismarck's bit and in 1890 he sacked the long-serving and experienced minister. With Willie now in charge of Germany, Europe careered towards World War I.

37. Vicky was a widow at forty-seven with no future role to play.

Vicky built herself a new home in the beautiful Taunus Hills of west Germany, far away from her son's capital in Berlin. She called it Friedrichshof (or Friedrich's House), as a memorial to her beloved husband. She knew the area well as she had stayed nearby during the Franco-Prussian War. She loved it because it reminded her of Scotland and Balmoral, where Fritz had proposed. Friedrichshof was built to the highest standards of comfort and the latest up-to-date design.

The failed Battenberg marriage

During his short reign as kaiser, the mortally ill Fritz gave his consent for the marriage of his second daughter Viktoria (born 1866) to Prince Alexander (Sandro) of Battenberg (1857-1893). He did so at the urging of Vicky and against his own better judgement. Viktoria (known in the family as Moretta) had been in love with Sandro for years and was encouraged by her mother in a desire to marry him. But such a marriage was viscerally opposed by Bismarck and the new kaiser Willie on both political and personal grounds.

The political grounds related to Sandro's brief tenure as sovereign prince of a newly independent state of Bulgaria. He was elected by the national assembly in 1879 but soon fell foul of powerful Russia and was forced to abdicate in 1886. The Prussian and Russian royal families were related and Bismarck had no desire to upset such a powerful ally.

The personal grounds related to Sandro's lack of royal status. His father (a prince of Hesse-Darmstadt) had married outside the royal circle so that Sandro and his brothers were not permitted to take their father's rank and titles. Such distinctions did not bother Victoria; one of Sandro's brothers married her daughter Beatrice and another her granddaughter (see chapter 8). But in Prussia they were taken very seriously.

Whilst Victoria saw no problem with the marriage on personal grounds, she recognised that the marriage would never be agreed to by Bismarck. She also sensed that as the years passed perhaps Sandro was losing interest. She cautioned her daughter not to push things too far, but Vicky would not listen. She continued to press for the marriage and, after Fritz's death, tried to twist her son Willie's arm by claiming this was the dying wish of his father.

Eventually the news reached Moretta that Sandro was living with the opera singer Johanna Loisinger whom he married in 1889. The following year (1890) Moretta married Adolf of Schaumburg-Lippe, a younger son from another German royal house. It seems likely she accepted him in desperation not to stay a spinster. After Adolf's death she caused a scandal by marrying a commoner called Alexander Zoubkov who was more than thirty years her junior. He quickly spent most of her money and then abandoned her.

From a young bride, Vicky was vocal about the discomfort of living in a German palace. In her first married home in Berlin there were no bathrooms or toilets, and she had to walk through the death chamber of a previous king of Prussia to reach her bedroom. Friedrichshof was lit by electricity, had en-suite bathrooms with hot and cold water, and a lift. Instead of being some distance away, as was usual in royal palaces, the kitchens were located next door to the dining room, so the food arrived hot to the table.

38. Vainglorious, pompous, deluded, Willie referred to himself as the 'All-Highest'.

Vicky survived her mother by only six months. When Victoria died in January 1901, Vicky was already terminally ill with breast cancer. She concealed her illness and the cancer was only discovered when doctors examined her following a fall from her horse. Vicky's death was long drawn out and painful. For some reason, now incomprehensible, the German doctors would not give her large enough doses of morphine to do more than dull the pain for just a few minutes. The sentries guarding Friedrichshof asked to be moved farther away so that they could not hear Vicky screaming with the pain. She wrote to her daughter.

The terrible nights of agony are worse than ever, no rest, no peace. The tears rush down my cheeks when I am not shouting with pain. The injections of morphia dull the pains a little for about a quarter of an hour, sometimes not at all, then they rage again with renewed intensity, and make me wish I were safe in my grave, ... It is fearful to endure. My courage is quite exhausted.[5]

Vicky died at Friedrichshof on 5 August 1901. Her three younger daughters, with whom she had an excellent relationship, were with her as much as possible during the last difficult months of her life. Vicky called them 'my three sweet girls'. She left Friedrichshof to her youngest daughter Margarethe (Mossy) who had married into a local noble family. After World War II Mossy's family turned Friedrichshof into a luxury hotel where my husband and I have been fortunate enough to stay.

10

IN A HURRY TO
DEVELOP A PHOTOGRAPH
OR PAINT A FLOWER

As Victoria aged, she came to rely on Beatrice more and more. The queen never retired from her official duties and was still adamantly opposed to passing on responsibilities to her heir Bertie, the prince of Wales. In her declining years, Victoria developed cataracts and her eyesight failed making it difficult to read or write. She was dependant on her daughters or ladies-in-waiting to read papers and letters to her and dictate the answers. The largest burden fell on Beatrice who was constantly at Victoria's side and controlled access to her mother. Historians have shuddered at the thought that this strait-laced princess with her narrow education could have been advising her failing mother on state affairs. Victoria's official private secretary wrote.

> The most absurd mistakes occur ... Imagine Princess Beatrice trying to explain our policy in the East ... I may write out long precis, but they are often not read to Her Majesty as Princess Beatrice is in a hurry to develop a photograph or wants to

paint a flower for a bazaar ... When her sole means of reading despatches, precis, debates, etc, lies in Princess Beatrice, it is simply hopeless.[1]

But I suspect his comments show male prejudice and may have underestimated Beatrice's abilities. She was intelligent and determined. From a lifetime at her mother's side, Beatrice must surely have gained great experience on state affairs.

39. Beatrice controlled access to her aging mother.

Queen Victoria died at Osborne House on the Isle of Wight at 6.30pm on Tuesday, 22 January 1901. Her son-in-law, the duke of Argyll (Louise's husband Lorne) likened her last moments to those of a great ship going down. Lenchen, Louise, and Beatrice were with their mother at the end – her three daughters who had stayed in Britain to support

40. Victoria's death in 1901 was compared to a great ship going down.

her. Alice had died in Darmstadt more than twenty years before and Vicky was dying slowly and painfully from cancer at Friedrichshof.

After Victoria's death her three surviving daughters (Lenchen, Louise, and Beatrice) became less important members of the royal family. The focus of public interest shifted to the new King Edward VII, his children, and grandchildren. Beatrice was the most affected. She lost her role at the centre of the royal household and was left without a home. Lenchen and Louise had their own establishments, but Beatrice had always lived with her mother, even as a married woman. Bertie's decision to get rid of Osborne House, which he hated, by giving it to the nation was especially painful for Beatrice. She loved the Isle of Wight and regarded Osborne as her home. This was where she had married Liko and where he was buried. Victoria had appointed Beatrice as governor of the Isle of Wight.

Spreading the defective gene

In 1906 Beatrice's only daughter Victoria Eugenie (1887-1969) married King Alfonso XIII of Spain (1886-1941). Christened Victoria for her grandmother and Eugenie for her godmother ex-Empress Eugenie of France (wife of Napoleon III) she was usually known as Ena, another of her given names.

King Alfonso XIII was a posthumous baby (born after his father's death) and king of Spain from birth. He was initially interested in another of Victoria's granddaughters as a bride (Princess Patricia of Connaught). When she appeared indifferent to his charms he turned to Ena. Entranced by Ena's golden good looks, Alfonso insisted on marrying her despite warnings she could be a carrier of haemophilia. Beatrice was a known carrier (one of Ena's brothers had the disease) so there was a fifty percent chance that her daughter Ena also carried the defective gene. Ena was dazzled by Alfonso's proposal and the chance to become queen of Spain. She converted to Catholicism and gave up her place in the British succession to marry him.

Spain was an unstable monarchy. Ena's wedding day was marred by violence when a terrorist threw a bomb at their carriage. She arrived at the palace for her wedding reception in a wedding dress spattered with blood. Dynastic disaster struck twelve months later when Ena gave birth to a son. It was discovered when the baby was circumcised that he had haemophilia. Of Alfonso and Ena's five sons, only the fourth, Juan Count of Barcelona, was not disabled. Their second son became deaf at an early age; the third was stillborn; and the youngest also had haemophilia. Alfonso's love for Ena was shattered; he could not forgive her for the haemophilia of their sons.

Spain stayed neutral in World War I and its monarchy survived while others tumbled. But this was only a reprieve. The monarchy was deposed, and the royal family sent into exile in 1931. After this Ena and Alfonso lived apart. Ena returned to Spain only once, in 1968, for the christening of her great-grandson Felipe. She did not live long enough to see her grandson Juan Carlos (the son of Juan Count of Barcelona) restored as king of Spain in 1975. He abdicated in 2014, following a scandal over his lavish African hunting trip when his country languished in deep recession, and Felipe became king.

Bertie was not very sympathetic to his youngest sister Beatrice's plight. He still felt lingering resentment over how Beatrice had been indulged as a child, and jealousy that she was always close to their mother in a way he was not.

Beatrice spent the remaining forty years of her own life editing her mother's journals. Victoria began the life-long habit of keeping a daily journal (or diary) at the age of thirteen when, as Princess Victoria of Kent, she wrote the first entry on 1 August 1832 in a small book given to her by her mother. The last entry was dictated to her granddaughter Thora (Lenchen's daughter) on 13 January 1901, only nine days before she died. Victoria seems to have been aware of the historical importance of her journal but concerned that some parts were too private to go on record. On her death, she entrusted the journal to Beatrice

41. Ena's golden good looks entranced the king of Spain.

with instructions to edit it for posterity. Starting with the entries for 1837, when her mother ascended the throne, Beatrice began the Herculean task of transcribing the journal. She amended or omitted anything she considered sensitive and destroyed the original volumes as she went. Out went references to John Brown and, who knows, perhaps also to her sister Louise's baby. At the end there were one hundred and eleven volumes in Beatrice's handwriting. Only thirteen of the original volumes in Victoria's handwriting survive, covering the period before she came to the throne. Beatrice's nephew, King George

V, was not happy about the loss of what he knew were irreplaceable historical documents but felt unable to stop his aunt since Beatrice was only doing what her mother had instructed.

Beatrice's published work shows her to be a skilled editor. Her last literary project was a book of translated extracts from the private diaries of her German great-grandmother, Duchess Augusta of Saxe-Coburg-Saalfeld (1757-1831). The duchess was a formidable woman, matriarch of the glamourous Saxe-Coburg royal clan, and the grandmother of both Victoria and Albert. The extracts Beatrice selected cover the turbulent years of the Napoleonic Wars. Published in 1941, Beatrice felt they had some resonance during the dark days of World War II. She was right: Duchess Augusta's opening words, written in April 1806, refer to the despotism of Napoleon but could equally apply to Hitler.

> The moon shines cold and bright in a cloudless sky. The mild breath of Spring has given way to cold biting east winds. It seems as if nature had allied itself with humanity to destroy all thoughts of happiness. There are nothing but storms in the atmosphere and amongst men. Poor Germany, what will thy fate yet be, given over to the caprices of a despot, who recognises no law but his own will, who sets no limit to his own lust for power, and to whom all means are justifiable to gratify this passion.[2]

Beatrice was the last of Queen Victoria's daughters. She died at Brantridge Park in West Sussex on 26 October 1944. This was the home of her niece (her brother Leopold's daughter). Beatrice's wartime funeral at St George's Chapel, Windsor Castle was attended by Queen Elizabeth (consort of George VI) and her eighteen-year-old daughter Princess Elizabeth (the future Queen Elizabeth II). Beatrice was a link between one great queen (Queen Victoria) and another (Queen Elizabeth II). The following year her remains were transferred to Whippingham Church on the Isle of Wight where she rests next to her husband Liko in their marble tomb in the Battenberg chapel.

11

QUEEN VICTORIA'S GRANDDAUGHTERS

The story of Queen Victoria and her daughters goes on through their descendants, many of whom also led fascinating and turbulent lives. There is so much more of the story still to tell. Vicky's daughter Sossy (Sophie) became queen of Greece; Alice's daughter Alicky (Alix) was tsarina of Russia; and Beatrice's daughter Ena (Victoria Eugenie) queen of Spain. Victoria's granddaughters were the trophy brides of their day and in all five became queen consorts. A sixth married the heir to the Swedish throne but died young before he became king. This was Princess Margaret of Connaught (Daisy) the daughter of Victoria's third son Arthur.

In 1889 Princess Sophie of Prussia (Sossy) married Constantine (Tino), heir to the throne of the Hellenes (Greece). Sossy was one of Vicky's 'three sweet girls' – the three daughters with whom she enjoyed a close relationship. Sossy's decision to convert to Greek Orthodoxy, the faith of her new country, caused a blazing row with her brother Willie (Kaiser Wilhelm II) who tried to ban her from visiting Germany.

Victoria's granddaughters who became queens

Tsarina Alexandra Feodorovna of Russia (1872-1918)
Born Alix of Hesse-Darmstadt (Alicky), the fourth daughter of Alice
Married 1894 Tsar Nikolai II of Russia (Nicky)
Five children: four girls and one boy
Murdered 1918 Ekaterinburg Russia

Queen Maud of Norway (1869-1938)
Born Maud of Wales (Harry), the youngest daughter of Bertie
Married 1896 Prince Carl of Denmark
King Haakon VII and Queen Maud of Norway from 1905
One child: a boy
Died 1938 London

Queen Victoria Eugenie of Spain (1887-1969)
Born Victoria Eugenie (Ena) of Battenberg, the only daughter of Beatrice
Married 1906 King Alfonso XIII of Spain
Deposed and exiled from Spain 1931
Six children: two girls and four boys
Died 1969 Lausanne Switzerland

Queen Sophie of Greece (1870-1932)
Born Sophie of Prussia (Sossy), the third daughter of Vicky
Married 1889 Crown Prince Constantine (Tino) of the Hellenes (Greece)
King Constantine I and Queen Sophie 1913-1917 and again 1920-1922
Six children: three girls and three boys
Died 1932 Frankfurt Germany

Queen Marie of Romania (1875-1938)
Born Marie of Edinburgh (Missy), the daughter of Victoria's son Affie
Married 1893 Crown Prince Ferdinand of Romania
King Ferdinand and Queen Marie of Romania from 1914
Six children: three girls and three boys
Died 1938 Sinaia Romania

Sossy's husband became King Constantine I in 1913 when his father, King George I, was assassinated. Greece was a shaky monarchy; Constantine I would be deposed during World War I, restored after the war, and then deposed again.

Princess Marie of Edinburgh (Missy) was the daughter of Victoria's second son. Missy turned down the chance to be queen of Great Britain by refusing a marriage proposal from the future King George V. This was at the bidding of her mother, a Russian grand duchess who hated playing second fiddle in Britain. Instead, Missy was married off at seventeen in 1893 in a loveless match to the rather ugly and boring Crown Prince Ferdinand of Romania.

42. Missy of Romania in typically theatrical pose
with her youngest daughter Ileana.

Missy was initially very unhappy in Romania but came to love her adopted country where her flamboyant personality made her hugely popular. Missy had love affairs and is rumoured to have given birth to two children who were not her husband's. But Ferdinand came to respect his wife's intelligence and contribution to Romania; they formed a good working partnership. They became king and queen of Romania in October 1914 just after the outbreak of World War I.

43. Queen Maud of Norway with her husband
King Haakon and son Crown Prince Olav.

Bertie's youngest daughter Princess Maud of Wales was an unlikely success story as queen of Norway. Bertie's wife Alix (Alexandra) treated her daughters as if they were much younger than their ages, and the three Wales girls were considered plain and childish. Maud, known as

Harry, was a tomboy who loved outdoor sports such as riding, cycling, and skating. In 1896, at the late age of twenty-six for a princess, Maud married Prince Carl of Denmark, a cousin she had known since childhood (his father and her mother were brother and sister). Rumour has it that their only child (a son born in 1903) was conceived by artificial insemination. Maud was reluctant to move to Denmark and preferred to stay at Appleton House on the Sandringham estate, a wedding present from her father.

In 1905 Carl was elected king of Norway (newly independent from Sweden) as King Haakon VII. Maud became a respected and popular queen of Norway where her unassuming manner and love of skiing and winter sports endeared her to Norwegians. She is famous for her fashion sense and for her slim figure. With the aid of corsets her waist measured a tiny eighteen inches (forty-five centimetres).

The marriage of Princess Alix of Hesse-Darmstadt (Alicky) to Tsar Nikolai II of Russia (Nicky) was a great success on the personal level but devastating for the Russian monarchy. Alicky was the youngest surviving daughter of Alice and given the name Alix because it was difficult to pronounce her mother's name in German. As a six-year-old Alix was traumatised by the diphtheria epidemic that claimed the lives of her mother and sister (see chapter 7). All the little girl's familiar toys were taken away and burned for fear of infection. She grew up to be ethereally beautiful but shy, self-conscious, and narrow minded. Her marriage to Nicky in 1894 was against the advice of her grandmother. Victoria distrusted Russia and could see that Alicky was entirely unsuited for the great public role of tsarina. Nor were Nicky's parents enthusiastic; they were aware of the risk that Alix could bring haemophilia into the Russian royal family (her mother Alice was a carrier). But Nicky was adamant he would marry no-one else.

The new tsarina was disliked by the Russian royal family and unpopular with the Russian people. They called her *the funeral bride* because her wedding to Nicky was only a week after his father's funeral. Alicky gave birth to four daughters in a row and when the longed-for son and heir finally arrived the tiny baby began bleeding through the navel. He had haemophilia! A mother's guilt at having passed on this terrible affliction led Alicky to rely on a deplorable mystic called Rasputin in the desperate fight to keep her son alive. Blind determination to hand over the Russian monarchy intact to her frail son drove her to stiffen Nicky's resolve against any reform. In World War I Nicky was away at the front and Alicky governed on his behalf. Hatred for her in Russia deepened; she was called *the German woman* and accused of treachery.

44. Alicky with her husband Nicky; she was unsuited in character to the great public role of tsarina of Russia.

When World War I began in 1914 Victoria's grandchildren sat on seven European thrones – Great Britain, Russia, Germany, Romania, Greece, Spain, and Norway (chart 6). Cousins from the Saxe-Coburg family were kings of two more countries – Belgium and Bulgaria. The catastrophic conflict would slaughter millions, pit royal cousin against cousin, and topple thrones. Bertie's son Georgie (King George V of Great Britain) was in alliance with his cousin Nicky in Russia (Tsar Nikolai II). Both the tsar and tsarina were Georgie's first cousins. Against them was their cousin Willie (Vicky's son Kaiser Wilhelm II of Germany). Two more cousins lined up with Willie as sovereigns of the German states (not shown on chart 6) – Alice's son Ernie (Ernst Ludwig) as grand duke of Hesse-Darmstadt and Leopold's son Charlie (Karl Eduard) as duke of Saxe-Coburg and Gotha.

At the urging of his wife Missy, King Ferdinand of Romania eventually joined the allies (her cousins in Great Britain and Russia) in 1916. Romania was then invaded but the king and queen resolutely defended a corner of their country and Missy became even more popular in her tireless heroism. After the war Ferdinand and Missy were crowned king and queen in one of the most theatrical coronations in history (designed by Missy). In Greece Sossy was relentlessly calumnied by the allies for her German birth and accused of adversely influencing her husband. King Constantine I tried unsuccessfully to maintain

45. Sossy's Prussian origins made her unpopular in Greece.

Greece's neutrality. He was deposed and exiled in 1917 when Greece joined the allies. Their second son Alexander took over the throne but died from an infected monkey bite in 1920. Constantine I was restored, but only briefly. Norway and Spain maintained their neutrality throughout the conflict. King Alfonso XIII's humanitarian work for prisoners-of-war on both sides was important enough to earn him nomination for the Nobel peace prize.

Exhausted by war losses and starved by food shortages, Russia erupted into revolution in March 1917. Nicky was forced to abdicate.

With Alicky and their five children, he was detained under house arrest, first at their palace near St Petersburg but later under far less favourable conditions in Siberia. Their lives were ended by savage butchery in a cellar in Ekaterinburg in July 1918. To his credit Alfonso XIII had tried to save his wife's relatives by negotiating with the Bolsheviks to offer Nicky and his family sanctuary in Spain. Willie and the other German cousins also lost their thrones (but not their lives) when revolution came to Germany in November 1918 and the German princes were forced to abdicate. Willie lived out the rest of his life (he died in 1941) in luxurious exile in the Netherlands. I have never understood why he was spared prosecution as a war criminal! Cousin Georgie (King George V of Great

46. Cousin Georgie (King George of Great Britain) kept his throne.

Britain) kept his throne. He had initially offered a home to his Russian cousins after Nicky's abdication but soon backed out when it became clear that harbouring a perceived tyrant like the tsar in Britain could put his own throne at risk.

Thrones continued to topple after World War II. The last king of Romania was Missy's grandson King Michael who was ousted by a communist regime in 1947. The Greek monarchy staggered on until Sossy's grandson King Constantine II fled the country in 1967. Descendants of Queen Victoria sit on four thrones today (chart 7). The king of Norway (Harald V) is Queen Maud's grandson; the king of Spain (Felipe VI) the great-grandson of Queen Ena; and the king of Sweden (Carl XVI Gustaf) the grandson of Princess Margaret of Connaught (Daisy) who died before her husband succeeded to the Swedish throne. King Charles III of Great Britain is the great-grandson of Georgie (King George V). Charles succeeded to the throne in September 2022 on the death of one of Britain's greatest monarchs – his mother Queen Elizabeth II.

CHARTS AND FAMILY TREES

1. Queen Victoria's children
2. The family of Vicky and Fritz
3. The family of Alice and Louis
4. The family of Lenchen and Christian
5. The family of Beatrice and Liko
6. The thrones descended from Queen Victoria on the outbreak of World War I
7. The thrones descended from Queen Victoria today

1. QUEEN VICTORIA'S CHILDREN

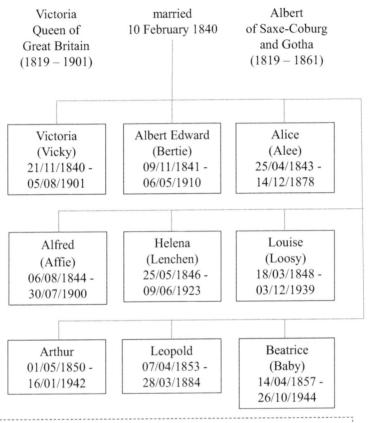

Victoria	married	Albert
Queen of	10 February 1840	of Saxe-Coburg
Great Britain		and Gotha
(1819 – 1901)		(1819 – 1861)

Victoria
(Vicky)
21/11/1840 -
05/08/1901

Albert Edward
(Bertie)
09/11/1841 -
06/05/1910

Alice
(Alee)
25/04/1843 -
14/12/1878

Alfred
(Affie)
06/08/1844 -
30/07/1900

Helena
(Lenchen)
25/05/1846 -
09/06/1923

Louise
(Loosy)
18/03/1848 -
03/12/1939

Arthur
01/05/1850 -
16/01/1942

Leopold
07/04/1853 -
28/03/1884

Beatrice
(Baby)
14/04/1857 -
26/10/1944

Chart shows the nine children of Queen Victoria and Prince Consort Albert, with their dates of birth and death and family nicknames.

2. THE FAMILY OF VICKY AND FRITZ

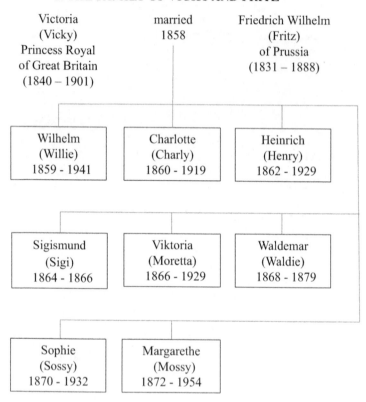

Victoria (Vicky) Princess Royal of Great Britain (1840 – 1901)	married 1858	Friedrich Wilhelm (Fritz) of Prussia (1831 – 1888)

Wilhelm (Willie) 1859 - 1941	Charlotte (Charly) 1860 - 1919	Heinrich (Henry) 1862 - 1929

Sigismund (Sigi) 1864 - 1866	Viktoria (Moretta) 1866 - 1929	Waldemar (Waldie) 1868 - 1879

Sophie (Sossy) 1870 - 1932	Margarethe (Mossy) 1872 - 1954

Chart shows the eight children of Queen Victoria's eldest daughter Vicky, with their dates of birth and death and family nicknames.

3. THE FAMILY OF ALICE AND LOUIS

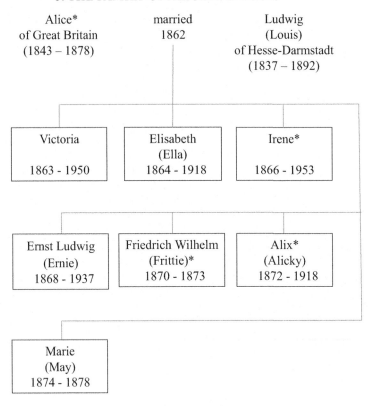

Alice*
of Great Britain
(1843 – 1878)

married
1862

Ludwig
(Louis)
of Hesse-Darmstadt
(1837 – 1892)

| Victoria 1863 - 1950 | Elisabeth (Ella) 1864 - 1918 | Irene* 1866 - 1953 |

| Ernst Ludwig (Ernie) 1868 - 1937 | Friedrich Wilhelm (Frittie)* 1870 - 1873 | Alix* (Alicky) 1872 - 1918 |

| Marie (May) 1874 - 1878 |

Chart shows the seven children of Queen Victoria's second daughter Alice, with their dates of birth and death and family nicknames. An asterisk * indicates those known to have been affected by haemophilia.

4. THE FAMILY OF LENCHEN AND CHRISTIAN

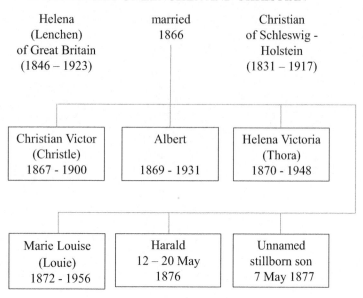

Helena   married   Christian
(Lenchen)   1866   of Schleswig -
of Great Britain   Holstein
(1846 – 1923)   (1831 – 1917)

Christian Victor (Christle) 1867 - 1900	Albert 1869 - 1931	Helena Victoria (Thora) 1870 - 1948
Marie Louise (Louie) 1872 - 1956	Harald 12 – 20 May 1876	Unnamed stillborn son 7 May 1877

Chart shows the five children of Queen Victoria's third daughter Lenchen, with their dates of birth and death and family nicknames. Chart also shows Lenchen's unnamed stillborn son.

5. THE FAMILY OF BEATRICE AND LIKO

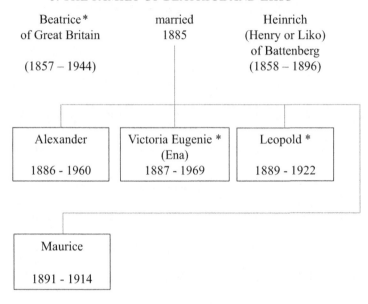

| Beatrice *
of Great Britain

(1857 – 1944) | married
1885 | Heinrich
(Henry or Liko)
of Battenberg
(1858 – 1896) |

| Alexander

1886 - 1960 | Victoria Eugenie *
(Ena)
1887 - 1969 | Leopold *

1889 - 1922 |

| Maurice

1891 - 1914 |

Chart shows the four children of Queen Victoria's fifth and youngest daughter Beatrice, with their dates of birth and death and family nicknames. An asterisk * indicates those known to have been affected by haemophilia.

6. THE THRONES DESCENDED FROM QUEEN VICTORIA
On the outbreak of World War 1

Queen Victoria

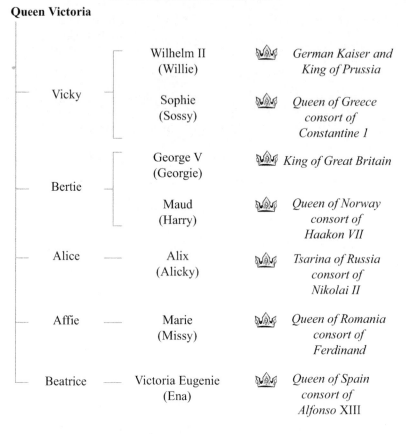

Chart shows the descent from Queen Victoria of her grandchildren who sat on European thrones (either as sovereign or consort) at the outbreak of World War I in 1914. It shows that the monarchs of seven countries were closely related to each other as first cousins

7. THE THRONES DESCENDED FROM QUEEN VICTORIA
Today

Queen Victoria

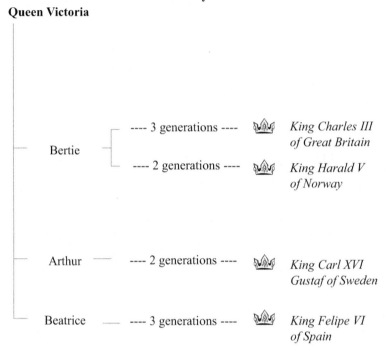

Bertie

---- 3 generations ---- *King Charles III of Great Britain*

---- 2 generations ---- *King Harald V of Norway*

Arthur ---- 2 generations ---- *King Carl XVI Gustaf of Sweden*

Beatrice ---- 3 generations ---- *King Felipe VI of Spain*

Chart shows the four European monarchs today who are descended from Queen Victoria

NOTES

Chapter 2. The five daughters of Queen Victoria

1. Cecil Woodham-Smith, *Queen Victoria: Her Life and Times, Volume 1 1819-1861*. London: Hamish Hamilton, 1972, 217.
2. Hannah Pakula, *An Uncommon Woman: The Empress Frederick, Daughter of Queen Victoria, Wife of the Crown Prince of Prussia, Mother of Kaiser Wilhelm*. London: Weidenfeld & Nicolson, 1996, 28.
3. Daphne Bennett, *King Without a Crown: Albert, Prince Consort of England 1819-1861*. Philadelphia: J B Lippincott, 1977, 304. Letter from Prince Albert to Vicky, 2 February 1858.
4. Roger Fulford (edited), *Dearest Child: Private Correspondence of Queen Victoria and the Crown Princess of Prussia 1858-1861*. London: Evans Brothers, 1964, 78. Letter from Queen Victoria to Vicky, 15 March 1858.
5. Jerrold M Packard, *Victoria's Daughters*. New York: St Martin's Press, 1998, 52.
6. Roger Fulford (edited), *Dearest Mama: Private Correspondence of Queen Victoria and the Crown Princess of Prussia 1861-1864*. London: Evans Brothers, 1968, 311. Letter from Queen Victoria to Vicky, 23 March 1864.
7. Queen Victoria's Journals, RA VIC/MAIN/QVJ (W) 18 March 1853 (Princess Beatrice's copies). Retrieved 1 January 2023.
8. Jehanne Wake, *Princess Louise: Queen Victoria's Unconventional Daughter*. London: Collins, 1988, 44.
9. Roger Fulford (edited), *Your Dear Letter: Private Correspondence of Queen Victoria and the German Crown Princess 1865-1871*. London: Evan Brothers, 1971, 114. Letter from Queen Victoria to Vicky, 9 January 1867.
10. David Duff, *The Shy Princess: The Life of Her Royal Highness Princess Beatrice, the Youngest Daughter and Constant Companion of Queen Victoria*. London: Evan Brothers, 1985, 25.
11. Ibid, 29.

Chapter 3. If the princess can leave the Englishwoman at home

1. Christopher Hibbert (edited), *Queen Victoria in Her Letters and Journals: A Selection by Christopher Hibbert*. New York: Viking, 1985, 98. Memorandum by the queen, 29 September 1855.
2. Ibid, 100. Letter from Queen Victoria to Lord Clarendon, 25 October 1857.
3. Pakula, *An Uncommon Woman*, 69-70. Letter from Count Otto von Bismarck to General Leopold von Gerlach at the time of Vicky and Fritz's engagement.
4. Frederick Ponsonby (edited). *Letters of The Empress Frederick*. London: Macmillan, 1928, 266.

5. Fulford (edited), *Your Dear Letter*, 77. Letter from Vicky to her mother, 19 June 1866.

6. Roger Fulford (edited), *Beloved Mama: Private Correspondence of Queen Victoria and the German Crown Princess 1878-1885*. London: Evan Brothers, 1981, 38. Letter from Vicky to her mother, 27 March 1879.

Chapter 4. More a funeral than a wedding

1. Gerard Noel, *Princess Alice: Queen Victoria's Forgotten Daughter*. London: Constable, 1984, 249. Letter from Alice to Florence Nightingale, 16 December 1872.

2. Fulford (edited), *Dearest Mama*, 85. Letter from Queen Victoria to Vicky, 2 July 1862 (the day after Alice's wedding).

3. Noel, *Princess Alice*, 120. Letter from Queen Victoria to King Leopold of the Belgians, 25 October 1865.

4. Fulford (edited), *Dearest Mama*, 85. Letter from Queen Victoria to Vicky, 2 July 1862.

5. Elizabeth Longford (edited), *Darling Loosy: Letters to Princess Louise, 1856-1939*. London: Weidenfeld & Nicholson, 1991, 147. Letter from Queen Victoria to Louise, 28 April 1871.

6. Fulford (edited), *Dearest Child*, 115. Letter from Queen Victoria to Vicky, 15 June 1858.

7. Princess Helena of Great Britain and Ireland, *Alice, Grand Duchess of Hesse, Princess of Great Britain and Ireland: Biographical Sketch and Letters*. London: John Murray, 1884, 243. Letter from Queen Victoria to Alice, 26 July 1870.

8. Noel, *Princess Alice*, 223-224. Letter from Alice to her husband Louis, 3 October 1876.

9. Princess Helena, *Alice, Grand Duchess of Hesse*, 305. Letter from Alice to her mother, 9 June 1873.

Chapter 5. When your parent and your sovereign settles a thing

1. George Earle Buckle (edited), *The Letters of Queen Victoria: A Selection from her Majesty's Correspondence and Journal Between the Years 1862 and 1878*. London: John Murray, 1926, volume 1, 85. Letter from Queen Victoria to King Leopold of the Belgians, 18 May 1863.

2. Fulford (edited), *Your Dear Letter*, 42. Letter from Queen Victoria to Vicky, 11 September 1865.

3. Buckle (edited), *The Letters of Queen Victoria*, 85. Letter from Queen Victoria to King Leopold of the Belgians, 18 May 1863.

4. Fulford (edited), *Your Dear Letter*, 50-51. Letter from Queen Victoria to Vicky, 23 December 1865.

5. Ibid, 86. Letter from Queen Victoria to Vicky, 1 August 1866.
6. Coryne Hall, *Princesses on the Wards: Royal Women in Nursing through Wars and Revolutions*. Stroud: The History Press, 2014, 30.
7. Susan Kay-Williams, *An Unbroken Thread: Celebrating 150 years of the Royal School of Needlework*. ACC Art Books, 2022, 12.
8. Princess Marie Louise, *My Memories of Six Reigns*. London: Evans Brothers Limited, 1956, 112.

Chapter 6. She is so very much admired
1. Fulford (edited), *Dearest Mama*, 311. Letter from Queen Victoria to Vicky, 23 March 1864.
2. Wake, *Princess Louise*, 78.
3. Ibid, 99.
4. Ibid, 107.
5. Buckle (edited), *The Letters of Queen Victoria: Between the Years 1862 and 1878*, volume 1, 632-633. Letter from Queen Victoria to her son Bertie (the prince of Wales), 29 November 1869.

Chapter 7. This dear, tender-hearted, noble-minded, sweet child
1. Noel, *Princess Alice*, 237. Letter from Alice to her mother, 15 November 1878.
2. Ibid, 239. Quoting Hansard (the record of what was said in parliament) of 17 December 1878.
3. Princess Helena, *Alice, Grand Duchess of Hesse*, 376.
4. Queen Victoria's Journals, RA VIC/MAIN/QVJ (W) 14 December 1878 (Princess Beatrice's copies). Retrieved 22 January 2023.

Chapter 8. I hope and pray there may be no results!
1. Fulford (edited), *Beloved Mama*, 186. Letter from Queen Victoria to Vicky, 25 April 1885.
2. Ibid, 177. Letter from Queen Victoria to Vicky, 7 January 1885.
3. Duff, *The Shy Princess*, 174.
4. Ibid, 172.

Chapter 9. The tragedy for my poor child is too ghastly
1. Pakula, *An Uncommon Woman*, 462.
2. Ponsonby (edited), *Letters of The Empress Frederick*, 326. Letter from Vicky to her mother, 5 July 1888.
3. Fulford (edited), *Your Dear Letter*, 82. Letter from Queen Victoria to Vicky, 28 July 1866.
4. Fulford (edited), *Dearest Child*, 13.

5. Pakula, *An Uncommon Woman*, 590.

Chapter 10. In a hurry to develop a photograph or paint a flower
1. Matthew Dennison, *The Last Princess: The Devoted Life of Queen Victoria's Youngest Daughter.* London: Weidenfeld & Nicolson, 2007, 205. Letter from Queen Victoria's official private secretary Frederick Ponsonby to his mother.
2. Augusta, Duchess of Saxe-Coburg-Saalfeld, *In Napoleonic Days: Extracts from the Private Diary of Augusta, Duchess of Saxe-Coburg-Saalfeld, Queen Victoria's maternal grandmother, 1806-1821: Selected and Translated by H.R.H. The Princess Beatrice.* London: John Murray, 1941, 1.

SELECTED BIBLIOGRAPHY

Baird, Diana. *Victorian days and a Royal Friendship.* Worcester: Littlebury and Company Ltd, 1985.

Benson, E.F. *Daughters of Queen Victoria.* London: Cassell, 1939.

Chomet, Seweryn. *Helena Princess Reclaimed: The Life and Times of Queen Victoria's Third Daughter.* New York, Begell House Inc, 1999.

Dennison, Matthew. *The Last Princess: The Devoted Life of Queen Victoria's Youngest Daughter.* London: Weidenfeld & Nicolson, 2007.

Duff, David. *The Shy Princess: The Life of Her Royal Highness Princess Beatrice, the Youngest Daughter and Constant Companion of Queen Victoria.* London: Evan Brothers, 1985.

Duff, David. *The Life Story of H.R.H. Princess Louise Duchess of Argyll.* Bath: Cedric Chivers Ltd, 1971.

Epton, Nina. *Victoria and Her Daughters.* London: Weidenfeld & Nicolson, 1971.

Fulford, Roger (edited). *Dearest Child: Private Correspondence of Queen Victoria and the Crown Princess of Prussia 1858-1861.* London: Evans Brothers, 1964. *Dearest Mama: Private Correspondence of Queen Victoria and the Crown Princess of Prussia 1861-1864.* London: Evans Brothers, 1968. *Your Dear Letter: Private Correspondence of Queen Victoria and the German Crown Princess 1865-1871.* London: Evan Brothers, 1971. *Darling Child: Private Correspondence of Queen Victoria and the German Crown Princess 1871-1878.* London: Evans Brothers, 1976. *Beloved Mama: Private Correspondence of Queen Victoria and the German Crown Princess 1878-1885.* London: Evan Brothers, 1981.

Golden, Robert. 'And Finally: The Royal World as Seen Through the Eyes of Robert Golden.' *Majesty: The Quality Royal Magazine.* Volume 41 number 8 and volume 43, numbers 9 and 11.

Hall, Coryne. *Princesses on the Wards: Royal Women in Nursing through Wars and Revolutions.* Stroud: The History Press, 2014.

Hall, Coryne. 'Princess Beatrice, the Isle of Wight's True Friend.' *Royalty Digest 3 2015.* Falkoping: Rosvall Royal Books, 2015, 8.

Hawksley, Lucinda. *The Mystery of Princess Louise: Queen Victoria's Rebellious Daughter.* London: Vintage Books, 2014.

Helena, Princess of Great Britain and Ireland. *Alice, Grand Duchess of Hesse, Princess of Great Britain and Ireland: Biographical Sketch and Letters.* London: John Murray, 1884.

Hibbert, Christopher (edited). *Queen Victoria in Her Letters and Journals: A Selection by Christopher Hibbert.* New York: Viking, 1985.

Hough, Richard (edited). *Advice to a Granddaughter: Letters from Queen Victoria to Princess Victoria of Hesse.* London: Heinemann, 1975.

Longford, Elizabeth (edited). *Darling Loosy: Letters to Princess Louise, 1856-1939.* London: Weidenfeld & Nicholson, 1991.

Marie Louise, Princess. *My Memories of Six Reigns.* London: Evans Brothers Limited, 1956.

Miller, Ilana. 'Grand Duke Serge Alexandrovitch (1857-1905).' *The Grand Dukes: Sons and Grandsons of Russia's Tsars since Paul 1, Volume I.* East Richmond Heights: Eurohistory.com, 2010.

Noel, Gerard. *Princess Alice: Queen Victoria's Forgotten Daughter.* London: Constable, 1984.

Packard, Jerrold M. *Victoria's Daughters.* New York: St Martin's Press, 1998.

Pakula, Hannah. *An Uncommon Woman: The Empress Frederick, Daughter of Queen Victoria, Wife of the Crown Prince of Prussia, Mother of Kaiser Wilhelm.* London: Weidenfeld & Nicolson, 1996.

Ponsonby, Frederick (edited). *Letters of The Empress Frederick.* London: Macmillan, 1928.

Queen Victoria. *Queen Victoria's Journals:* www.queenvictoriasjournals.org. Windsor: The Royal Archives, 2012.

Ramm, Agatha (edited). *Beloved and Darling Child: Last Letters Between Queen Victoria & Her Eldest Daughter 1886-1901.* Stroud: Sutton Publishing, 1998.

Sinclair, Andrew. *The Other Victoria: The Princess Royal and The Great Game of Europe.* London: Weidenfeld & Nicolson, 1981.

Stamp, Robert M. *Royal Rebels: Princess Louise and the Marquis of Lorne.* Toronto & Oxford: Dundern Press, 1988.

Van Der Kiste, John. *Dearest Vicky, Darling Fritz: The Tragic Love Story of Queen Victoria's Eldest Daughter and The German Emperor.* Stroud: Sutton Publishing, 2001.

Van Der Kiste, John. *Princess Helena: Queen Victoria's Third Daughter.* South Brent: A & F Publications, 2015.

Van Der Kiste, *Queen Victoria's Children.* Stroud: Sutton Publishing, 2003.

Wake, Jehanne. *Princess Louise: Queen Victoria's Unconvential Daughter.* London: Collins, 1988.

Woodham-Smith, Cecil. *Queen Victoria: Her Life and Times, Volume 1 1819-1861.* London: Hamish Hamilton, 1972.

Queen Victoria has a life story that is full of drama, intrigue, and surprises. She is the British monarch in history whose name everyone knows. Susan Symon's series of books focus on the queen as a woman – her personal life, events that formed her resolute character, and relationships that were important to her. They are illustrated throughout with portraits and memorabilia from the author's collection and use some of Victoria's own words, from her letters and journal, to help tell the story.

If you thought history was dull, this author will make you think again.
Roseland Arts Festival.

Young Victoria covers the bizarre events of Victoria's birth, when there was a scramble to produce the next heir to the throne; her lonely childhood under a tough regime; and the national adulation when she came to the throne aged eighteen. *Victoria & Albert* tells the story of one of the most famous relationships in history. There were early troubles with a personality clash and struggle for dominance in the relationship. They came through these to create a true partnership and found a dynasty.

The style is lively and the illustrations gorgeous. I highly recommend this book!
Amazon review.

THE COLOURFUL PERSONAL LIFE OF QUEEN VICTORIA

Victoria the Widowed Queen covers the long years of Victoria's widowhood when she became an icon of the age and matriarch of a huge clan. The first years as a widow were the least successful of her reign. She refused to appear in public and her popularity suffered. She gradually emerged from gloom but her seclusion in remote homes fuelled rumours about her private life. Her relationship with a servant caused scandal and later in life she had a puzzling relationship with a young Indian man.

Susan is on a mission to promote royal history to as many readers as possible.
Royalty Digest Quarterly Journal

Victoria's Daughters explores the stories of her five daughters, tinged with tragedy and scandal. Victoria had qualities that made her a great queen, but she was not at her best as a mother. The princesses were born into privilege and deference. But their lives were blighted by the early death of their father, Prince Albert, and dominated by the demands of their controlling mother. Her daughters were important public figures in their own time but are largely forgotten today.

Susan has done another fantastic job, proving that history can also be fun...
Eurohistory: The European Royal History Journal

QUEEN VICTORIA IN CORNWALL
THE ROYAL VISIT TO CORNWALL IN 1846

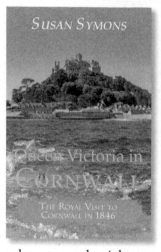

On the evening of Friday 4 September 1846, the royal yacht *Victoria and Albert* steamed into the harbour at Falmouth in Cornwall flying the royal standard. On board were Queen Victoria, her husband Prince Albert, and their two eldest children – five-year-old Vicky (Victoria, princess royal) and four-year-old Bertie (Albert Edward, prince of Wales).

Their arrival in Falmouth was part of the royal visit to Cornwall when Victoria came ashore to see the sights, meet the local aristocracy in their great houses, and patronise local industries.

Queen Victoria in Cornwall is an account of the queen's royal visit to Cornwall and follows in Victoria's footsteps to revisit the sights she saw. There was huge public interest in Victoria's young son. As the eldest son of the sovereign Bertie was the duke of Cornwall from birth and the first duke to visit Cornwall for two hundred years.

With colour illustrations, sketch maps, and family trees, the book should appeal to anyone who enjoys history, or follows royalty, or likes sightseeing in Cornwall.

Cover image:
St Michael's Mount, Cornwall (Miraphoto/Shutterstock)

THE SCHLOSS SERIES OF BOOKS

Schloss is the German word for castle or palace and you are never far from one of these in Germany. For most of its history Germany was not a single country but a patchwork of royal states, held together under the banner of the Holy Roman Empire. The dukes and princes who ruled these states were passionate builders. Their beautiful castles and palaces, and their compelling personal stories, provide the material for the *Schloss* series of books.

Each of the *Schloss* books includes twenty-five beautiful castles and palaces in Germany and looks at these from two aspects. The first is the author's experience as a visitor; the second, colourful stories of the historical royal families that built and lived in them.

Royalty were always the celebrities of their day and these royal stories from history can rival anything in *Hello* magazine. The *Schloss* books might encourage you to go and see these wonderful castles and palaces for yourself.

This book can be seen as an inspiration ... to get there and find the lesser known palaces and learn more about their history.
Royalty Digest Quarterly Journal.

Printed in Great Britain
by Amazon

27594592R00069